LIVING WRITERS

LIVING WRITERS

BEING CRITICAL STUDIES BROADCAST IN THE B.B.C. THIRD PROGRAMME BY

Denis Johnstone on Sean O'Casey

Arthur Calder-Marshall on Graham Greene

W. J. Turner on Christopher Isherwood

L. A. G. Strong on Elizabeth Bowen

Geoffrey Grigson on Wyndham Lewis

E. Sackville-West on I. Compton-Burnett

Rose Macaulay on E. M. Forster

V. S. Pritchett on George Orwell

Dylan Thomas on Walter de la Mare

Peter Quennell on Aldous Huxley

John Betjeman on Evelyn Waugh

Louis Marlow on T. F. Powys

with an essay on " The Written and the Spoken Word "
by the editor

GILBERT PHELPS

SYLVAN PRESS

WORDS ARE
OUR SUBTILLEST
AND DELICATEST
OUTWARD CREAT-
URES, BEING
COMPOSED OF
THOUGHTS
AND
BREATH

John Donne

CONTENTS

ACKNOWLEDGEMENTS

To the various contributors, for their co-operation.

To Mrs. W. J. Turner, for her kind permission for the inclusion of her late husband's talk on Christopher Isherwood.

For permission to use the copyright material I am indebted to the following :

Miss Elizabeth Bowen, Messrs. Constable & Co. Ltd. (for the extracts from " *The Last September* "), Messrs. Sidgwick & Jackson Ltd. (for the extracts from " *Ann Lee's* "), and Victor Gollancz Ltd. (for the extracts from " *To the North* " and " *The Death of the Heart* ").

Miss I. Compton-Burnett, Messrs. Wm. Heinemann Ltd. (for the extracts from " *Men and Wives* ", " *A House and Its Head* ") ; H. Cranton & Co. Ltd. (for the extract from " *Brothers and Sisters* ") ; Victor Gollancz Ltd. (for the extract from " *Daughters and Sons* ", " *Parents and Children* ", " *Elders and Betters* ").

Mr. Walter de la Mare, Messrs. Faber & Faber Ltd. (for the extracts from " *Crewe* ", " *On the Edge* ", " *Pleasures and Speculations* ", " *A Book of Words* ", " *The Scarecrow* ", " *Miss Duveen* "— from " *The Riddle and Other Stories* "), Messrs. Longman, Green & Co. Ltd. (for the extract from " *Seaton's Aunt* ", which appeared in " *The Mercury Story Book* ").

Mr. E. M. Forster, Messrs. Arnold & Co. Ltd. (for the extracts from " *Aspects of the Novel* ", " *The Longest Journey* ", " *Howard's End* ", " *Where Angels Fear to Tread* ", " *A Passage to India* "), Messrs. Sidgwick & Jackson Ltd. (for the extract from " *Writers of Today*, ed. by Denys Val Baker ").

Mr. Graham Greene, Messrs. Wm. Heinemann Ltd. (for the extracts from " *England Made Me* ", " *The Power and the Glory* ", " *Journey Without Maps* ", " *It's a Battlefield* "), and Messrs. Longman, Green & Co. Ltd. (for the extracts from " *The Lawless Roads* ").

Mr. Aldous Huxley, and Messrs. Chatto & Windus Ltd. (for the extracts from " *Crome Yellow* " and " *Vulgarity in Literature* ").

Mr. Christopher Isherwood, and the Hogarth Press (for the extracts from " *Sally Bowles* " and " *Lions and Shadows* ").

Mr. Wyndham Lewis, Messrs. Chatto & Windus Ltd. (for the extract from " *Time and Western Man* "), Messrs. Cassell & Co. Ltd. (for the extracts from " *Men Without Art* "), The Egoist Press, 1918 (for the extract from " *Tarr* "), The Oxford University Press (for the extracts from " *Essay on Objective·and Plastic Art in Our Time* ").

Mr. Sean O'Casey, and Messrs. Macmillan & Co. Ltd. (for the extracts from " *The Shadow of A Gunman* ", " *The Plough and the Stars* ", " *The Silver Tassie* ", " *Oakleaves and Lavender* ".

Mr. George Orwell, and the Hogarth Press (for the extract from an article in " *New Writing* "), Victor Gollancz Ltd. (for the extract from " *Burmese Days* ").

Mr. T. F. Powys, and Messrs. Chatto & Windus Ltd. (for the extracts from " *Soliloquies of A Hermit* ", " *John Pardy and the Waves* ", " *A Suet Pudding* " (both from " *Bottle's Path* "), and " The West Country Magazine" (for the extract from " *The Devil and the Good Deed* ").

Mr. Evelyn Waugh, and Messrs. Chapman & Hall Ltd. (for the extracts from " *Vile Bodies* ", " *Scoop* ", " *Work Suspended* ").

And also to Messrs. Arnold & Co. Ltd. (for the extracts from the late M. R. James' " *Canon Alberic's Scrap Book* " and " *A School Story* ").

PREFACE

" LIVING WRITERS " was the title of a series of talks
in which various writers were invited to speak about
their contemporaries. The talks were broadcast in the
Third Programme of the B.B.C. between October and
December, 1946, and also in the West of England Home
Service. Recently some of them have been repeated in
the Third Programme.

In planning a series of talks, twelve is usually the
limit if continuity of interest and unity of impression are
to be preserved and so it was decided that prose writers
only should be discussed, in these particular programmes.
As it is, there are startling gaps ; it might be objected
that a series that failed to make critical examination of the
work of George Bernard Shaw, for example, could
hardly claim to be representative of our contemporary
prose literature. But certain important contemporaries
were omitted in order that the series, in the scope of the
twelve talks, should include representatives of several
generations of writers, and illustrate various aspects of
modern literature.

Although all the talks were broadcast under the general
title of " Living Writers " there was, in fact, no serialisa-

tion in the sense that the various contributors " led into " each others' talks. The requirements of the Third Programme made it necessary that each should stand by itself. It was intended, however, that there should be some appearance of pattern in the series as a whole. For example, the talks were not restricted to writers of fiction : Sean O'Casey was included as a representative of modern drama. George Orwell is a prose writer who, although he does write novels, is pre-eminently (to quote from Mr. Pritchett's script) " a documentary writer, a kind of social anthropologist ".

At the same time it was the object of the series to illustrate, through the critical perceptions of different speakers, the various attitudes of the period ' in between the wars ', so that talks about Aldous Huxley, Wyndham Lewis, Christopher Isherwood, Evelyn Waugh, Graham Greene were clearly essential. Then there were writers of a very different outlook in Ivy Compton-Burnett, and Elizabeth Bowen. It was indispensable too that there should be talks about E. M. Forster, and about the prose work of Walter de la Mare.

" Living Writers " consisted of twelve programmes, each of twenty minutes. These talks are included in this book, with one exception. Mr. MacCarthy is writing about Sir Max Beerbohm in another context. There is also one addition to the original series. This is Louis Marlow's talk about Theodore Francis Powys, which was given in the second series of " Literature in the West ", and was broadcast in the West of England Home Service in the summer of 1946.

These talks, which are printed here in the order in which they were broadcast, were all illustrated by extracts from the works of the writers under discussion, read in most cases by professional readers. These quotations were an important feature of the broadcasts, and it is hoped that they will prove equally valuable to the reader.

The publishers are presenting this book to the public in the belief that these talks deserve to be preserved in book form, and because they feel that they will be as enjoyable to read as they were to listen to.

THE WRITTEN AND THE SPOKEN WORD

by GILBERT PHELPS

WHEN THE EDITOR of a series of talks watches those
words which were last heard over the microphone,
accompanied by all the inflections and gestures of the
speaker's personality, now lying down on the page in
orderly black and white, he cannot help thinking hard
about the relationship between the written and the
spoken word. What remains when the last echo of the
speaker's voice has been forgotten ? Is the marrow lost
in the transposition from microphone to printed page,
and only the dry bones of a talk left ? . . . This essay
is a purely personal attempt to answer these questions
and to examine some of the principles underlying them,
from the evidence provided by this particular series of
talks.

*　　*　　*　　*　　*

First of all, however, there were certain obvious
editorial problems to be faced. It is in meeting these
that one is brought on to more profound reflections.
For example—should a speaker be asked to revise his
script, in order to bring it closer to his ' literary ' style ?
Or should it be published exactly as it was spoken over
the microphone ?

A compromise seemed to emerge naturally and reasonably. Most of the abbreviations of colloquial speech have been turned back into ' written ' form. At the same time references to the microphone, and direct addresses to the ' listener ' have been avoided in this book, because it is irritating for the eye to be confronted by appeals to the ear.

A script often has to be thinned out in rehearsal, so that the sentences will reach the listener with a clearer ring. The contributors have in some cases restored cuts—not always though, because cutting often improves a script, both as a talk, and as a piece of writing. As Chekhov once said, the art of successful composition is a matter of removing from the coin everything that is not the head. There seemed no reason, however, why the more leisurely reader should not have the opportunity of reading passages that appeared in the original scripts, but which were cut in the actual broadcasts purely for considerations of timing.

Some of the contributors have made a few minor alterations, inserted an occasional word or sentence. For example, Mr. Pritchett has added a short paragraph to his talk on George Orwell, and Miss Rose Macaulay has included an additional short paragraph, which she inserted in the " Listener " version of her talk.*

In spite of these minor alterations however, the scripts remain substantially as they were when they were broadcast. The adjustments have not been sufficient to impair their interest as authentic examples of radio literary criticism, while they have made them more suitable for the reader. This does not mean, of course, that these scripts should be taken as examples of their writers' " literary style ". The critic, in each case, would

---

* " *The Listener* ", 12th *December*, 1946, *Vol. XXXVII*, *No.* 935.

have written differently, if he had addressed himself to a
reader and not to a listener. His angle of approach
would have been different ; he would have envisaged a
different audience ; he would have relied on the habits
of the reading eye, and written accordingly ; his style
would have been at once more discursive and more
" literary ". The reader, indeed, may find that some of
the sentences which were perfectly adapted to the
emphatic thrusts of the speaking voice, convey rather a
staccato effect when they are taken in by the eye. Some
of the longer periods too, broken up by frequent punctua-
tion and parenthesis, *look* untidy because of course they
were shaped to the twists and turns of the arguing voice,
or to the play of the speaker's personality.

All the same, in editing " Living Writers " for
publication, I found myself brought to the conclusion that
the differences between language designed for the eye and
language designed for the ear have been exaggerated. A
good radio talk is also a good script—that is, a good piece
of *writing*, however conscientiously the writer was
shaping his thoughts for the microphone. Otherwise,
there would be little justification for " The Listener ",
and certainly none for this book.

There is a school of thought, however, which claims
that a genuine radio script, by the very nature of its
language approach, must be unsuitable for reproduction
in print. The habits of the reading eye, it is said, are so
different from those of the ear, that no communion is
possible between them. One writer went so far as to
postulate two entirely separate functions of language.
" I believe " he wrote, " that language, like a plant with
two sexes, includes two principles of life ", and later he
claims " we all have at our command in our own right
two languages rather than one ".*

* " *Broadcasting, Speech and Writing* ", by *Christopher Salmon, printed in* " *The
Mint* ", *edited by Geoffrey Grigson (Routledge, 1946).*

If this is accepted, naturally it must follow that :—
" What may properly be attempted with language in speech is different from what may properly be written ; and what is required of language in prose is different from what speech requires ".

I cannot help feeling that this attempt to cut across the great living jet of our language, to drive it into separate compartments, is as futile as the efforts of the Logicians to classify the " Figures of Speech ". A language, like any other living organism, is a whole. Every attempt to split it up into separate functions, or separate kinds, every attempt to lop off pieces—which harden into ' journalese', or ' jargon ', or Basic English, or whatever it might be— is a dangerous interference, which, like a clot in the bloodstream, affects the vigorous flow.

It would be a tragedy indeed if radio, with its un- equalled opportunities for preserving and strengthening the integrity of language, erected the microphone into a magic cult with a private language of its own !

The essential unity of language is indeed implicit in in its origins. For fundamentally all language is based upon the spoken word, upon the rhythms and inflections of the speaking voice. As Newman said :—

" Properly speaking the terms by which we denote this characteristic gift of man, belong to its exhibition by means of the voice, not of handwriting. It addresses itself, in its primary idea, to the ear, not to the eye ".†

The transference of language from speech to the written word, certainly did nothing to break this unity. For in writing the derivation from speech is never forgotten. In writing, for example, we still use terms belonging to speech—such as ' saying ', ' speaking

---

† " *Literature : A Lecture in the School of Philosophy and Letters* " in " *The Idea of A University* ", by *John Henry Cardinal Newman* (*Longmans*, 1931, p. 273).

about ', ' calling '. In writing, we refer the words which we shape with our pens back to some recess of the mind where we *speak* them aloud. Thousands of little tongues move continually on the pulses of the imagination.

This recognition by the written word of its single origin in speech, emphasises the essential unity of language. That itself is a sufficiently exciting challenge to those engaged in broadcasting.

It is of course true that the range of the eye is in some ways wider than that of the ear. The eye can run ahead, and take into account the shape and layout of the page : anticipation and preparation, as I. A. Richards showed, play an important part in the pleasure of reading. But it would be an insult to the ear to suggest that its resources are limited to the apprehension of each single sound as it falls from a speaker or from the receiver set. The listener is not nearly as insulated as some people claim. The intelligent listener can do more than merely follow the thread of an argument. The reactions of the mind to language are not confined to a single sense; they are not bound by space or time. The ear too can make lightning decisions, it can make lightning acceptances, and rejections. It can collect impressions, arguments, and asides, and collate them—if not during the course of a talk, then some time *afterwards*.

The ear, in fact, is no more isolated than the eye, in its relation to the brain. Just as the reader or writer tests the evidence of his eye by the experience of his ear—so too the listener refers to the experience of the eye. It is impossible to say exactly which parts of any passage, written or spoken, affect exclusively the eye, or exclusively the ear. Their impressions and messages are very rapidly interchangeable. The eye and ear, in fact, are continuously checking and supplementing each other's experience. Or indeed the experience of any of the other senses. For, of all forms of expression, language is the most *inclusive*. It relies upon the testimony of all the senses more than any other medium. And this is particularly true in a " kinaesthetic " language like English.

If the eye and the ear, then, draw upon the same fund of experience, the " appropriate " language for each is fundamentally the same language. There is no inherent difference between the language used for the eye, and that addressed to the ear, even though there is usually a difference of emphasis. Indeed, when the two draw apart, it indicates a weakening or a lack of balance in any particular culture. An extreme example, leading to actual fracture, can be found in certain parts of Malaya, where the spoken language is at the simplest level of everyday economic requirements, while the " literary " language is practised only by a few pundits working in complete isolation. And it was the instinct of genius that led Wordsworth to emphasise the importance of " the language really used by men ", just at a time when the English language was showing signs of over-development in certain directions, and when some of its tissues were thickening into grossness. A continual interplay between the language of speech and that of the written word is essential for the well-being of language.

In actual fact of course the relationships between them vary considerably from age to age, and from individual to individual. There was a time when the two were almost identical, at least among the " educated ". Then in the self-contained society of the eighteenth century, the written and the spoken word again drew close. The brilliant conversation of the coffee houses became a habit which practice made into an art. The use of the title

" Discourses " for books is significant. " The Spectator "
was designed as a pattern of social speech and intercourse.
There is little difference between the language of Burke's
prose, and that of his parliamentary speeches.

. This revival of the Art of the spoken word was indeed
temporary. It belonged to a specialised culture, and the
narrowness of its social context led to pomposity and
over-stylisation. Wordsworth's attack on the " ornate
diction " of the late " Augustans " could be applied with
equal force to prose and speech, as to poetry. But the
tradition of brilliant conversation and its overflow into
prose survived, with varying degrees of literary success
in such writers as Lamb, Hazlitt, and Peacock, and has
never entirely died out.

The conditions of modern civilisation have, however,
made drastic encroachments upon the integrity of our
language. There are now vast bedraggled fringes, and
to these the serious writer or speaker can only apply the
scissors. And of course the spoken word, the language
of everyday intercourse, has been more vulnerable to
debasing influences than the written word. . . .

Unless, indeed, the process has been the other way
round—and the vulgarisation of the written word has
tarnished the spoken . . . When one reads the dignified
prose of some of the mid-Victorian periodicals, one
cannot escape the feeling that this is actually the *speech*
of the pulpit and the study. And one remembers
Coleridge's suggestion that everyday speech was itself
considerably influenced by these agencies.

Interactions between various sections of society are not
as easy now of course. But this is indeed the great
opportunity of broadcasting. What other agency has
the power of setting high standards, and of attempting
a new integration of language and culture ?

British broadcasting has faithfully tried to meet this challenge. There can be no doubt that the radio talk, for example, has substantially contributed to the improvement of speech, and to the raising of educational standards. Broadcasting in this country may yet revive the art of the spoken word, bringing its idiom closer to that of prose, and achieving that continuous intermingling of the written and the spoken word that is essential to the well being of language and culture. But, it cannot fulfil its great task effectively if it is charmed by the cult of the microphone into believing in a hybrid form of language, and so fails to realise that language like peace is indivisible.

It may be objected that a closer communion between the spoken and the written word would be detrimental to " literature " and to " style ". But some of the finest prose is easy and colloquial, and even the most highly-wrought has *some* relation to the spoken word. Even a deliberate experiment like Euphuism has some basis in an affectation or fashion of *speech*. And the most vivid Elizabethan prose—that of the pamphlets—is rich with the speech of the streets, the countryside and the market place. The more self-conscious prose of a later age was still an attempt to put on paper an idealised form of utterance. After all, most people write as they wish they could speak . . .

I am not overlooking the fact that much of the best prose is pitched in a higher key, which brings it on to the same level of intensity as poetry. But neither poetry nor " poetical " prose is using a " separate " language. Indeed the relationship of poetry to the speaking voice and to the ear is fundamental.

The nature of " style " in fact is too often misunderstood. As Newman said, " style is a thinking out into language ". It is only bad prose or bad speech that is littered with the bric à brac of " embellishment ". Images in language are not strings of fairy lights, placed for decoration. They are there for *illumination*. It is true that the reader is in some ways better equipped to appreciate the graces of style, and the significance of imagery. But the ear too can be responsive to subtleties and beauties of expression . . . " Style " is not something that belongs only to the written word, or that can be enjoyed only by the reader.

Imagery after all works through the ear in the same way as it does through the eye. In both cases there is a " delayed action ". The full significance may not be obvious exactly at the time of reading, or at the time of listening. Images in language are like those pellets of paper children play with—you drop them into a tumbler of water, and as they become saturated they open out into trails and clusters of blossoms.

In broadcasting there is a great future for the speaking of distinguished language, not only as ' readings ' from literature, but also as real and personal speech. Many broadcasters have, of course, seized this opportunity, and in this way much can be done in raising the levels of speech—and therefore of writing—throughout the country. Some broadcasters indeed can " get away " with uncompromisingly literary language over the microphone, through sheer force of personality. The style of Mr. Dylan Thomas's script on Walter de la Mare, for example, reveals very few concessions to " radio language ".

None of these arguments, it must be emphasised, in any way belittles the work of the radio expert. Any producer knows that certain words, and sentences, and grammatical forms, are difficult for the tongue to shape and for the ear to receive. Careful rehearsal can completely transform a script. Most people, when they first try to speak with conscious intention, have no real idea of the capacities or possibilities of their speaking voices. The producer's job is to help the speaker find his natural mode of utterance, and to bend his language into the contours of his personality. This process may be a beneficial one : for if a person speaks unnaturally, the odds are that he will write unnaturally, because he has not yet *thought* naturally.

An " outstanding " radio talk, however, is " good " long before it reaches the microphone. It was a good piece of writing in its draft script. Or, if not then, it was a good piece of writing, a sound use of language, in the broadcaster's mind, before, by a sudden jerk, he turned its direction towards the microphone instead of on to the printed page.

The *quality* of the thought, and therefore the quality of the language, is unchanged. The difference between the language of the spoken and that of the written word is one of degree, not of kind. Another lens is dropped into the telescope, which shifts the focus, bringing out certain details more vividly, but without changing the field of vision or the ' composition ' of the view.

For it must always be remembered that if the origin of all language is in the speaking voice, the *purpose* behind its invention was to express *thought*. Language was devised by man as a vehicle for ideas. Indeed to a large extent thinking *is* the use of words. For it is the act of formulation that *makes* the idea—that drags it out of the shadowy recesses of the mind and gives it shape and clarity.

Language is of course used to express emotions too— but language inevitably submits emotion to an *intellectual*

process. There was, no doubt, an adequate range of
sounds to express feelings long before the invention of
words. But emotion cannot be moulded into significant
artistic shape until it has passed through the intellectual
process and has been stamped with the right and inevitable
words. Then it may emerge—in a highly charged and
evocative form, indeed—but however impassioned and
' emotive ' the language, it is shaped and permeated by
thought.

Every form of expression is, after all, an endeavour to
reach truth, or some part of it. This applies as much to
prose and to speech, as it does to lyric poetry. A thought
or a feeling is not properly comprehended, or not
sufficiently important, if the mind is unable or unwilling
to submit it to the intellectual process, and so find the
right words for it. Language is being used falsely or
loosely when it strays away from this concern with
' truth '. As Hobbes so finely says :—

" Seeing then that *truth* consisteth in the right ordering
of names in our affirmations, a man that seeketh precise
truth, had need to remember what every name he uses
stands for ; and to place it accordingly, or else he will
find himself entangled in words, as a bird in lime-
twigges ".

Precision in the use of words, integrity of thought and
feeling, are perhaps even more important in Radio than
in print. The listener cannot answer back : and the
temptations to " slickness ", slipshod thinking and
statement are so vast.

Any proposal that Radio language is something
separate, that it creates " a fourth estate " in language, or
that its job is a new form of " suggestion " which debars
i t from hard thinking and precise statement, seems to me

lamentable. It may result in a blurring of the truth instead of clarification. It may lend itself too easily to propaganda, and emotional exploitation. The listener may find himself " entangled in words " that mean nothing.

Such a danger is not altogether imaginary. Beginners in Radio are sometimes offered " models " of Radio talking, which are in fact nothing more than collections of " microphone tricks " designed primarily to give play to the personality of the speaker. Radio personalities are of course pleasant, and "microphone tricks" certainly useful, but content is more important than " slickness " and ease of manner.

Now the talks presented in this book were given in the Third Programme of the B.B.C. The importance of the Third Programme is that it is independent of extraneous appeals and temptations. Its standards can be truly " objective "—that is, related wholly to the needs of the subject and the demands of truth.

Though the Third Programme has a different brief, however, it would be disastrous if it were considered as a " separate " organisation, lopped off from the rest of broadcasting. The Third Programme is not necessarily remote or academic : there is nothing it would like better than to see the size of its audiences steadily expanding. But its job is not to educate. Its function is rather that of an " Academy " :—to set up inside broadcasting the highest possible standards. But the same principles of integrity of thought and feeling, and honesty of intention apply to all broadcasting, or indeed to any medium that is not dominated by commercial considerations. They apply to drama, or variety, or music, as much as they do to the Third Programme.

The task of the broadcaster in the Third Programme is perhaps in some ways easier than that of other speakers. Freed from the necessity of so called " popularisation " he can develop his ideas in his own way. He can expect active co-operation from his listeners. He will be dealing with a stock of ideas, experiences, and intellectual habits which he and his listener hold more or less in common.

In talks written for the Third Programme, then, we may expect the gap between the spoken and the written word to be narrower. The speakers were of course aware that they were addressing themselves to the microphone, and not writing a " literary essay ". Their style is idiomatic and economical . . . But there is no hint, it seems to me, of any " different language ". I do not think, for example, that Mr. Grigson's talk on Wyndham Lewis, or Mr. Quennell's on Aldous Huxley, or Mr. V. S. Pritchett's on George Orwell, suffer any slackening of intention or impoverishment of content, because they are addressed primarily to the ear. I can see no hint that " suggestion " has replaced " statement " and precise thought.

In offering " Living Writers " to the public then, my own personal belief is that all these talks, though they were designed for the listener, will prove equally interesting and enjoyable to the reader. I believe too that they will illustrate the fundamental integrity of language, and its basis in thought and reason. Newman's famous remarks about speech and thought seem to me to form the ideal testament for all those who are concerned with the health of our English language and culture :

" Thought and speech are inseparable from each other. Matter and expression are parts of one : style is a thinking out into language . . . Call to mind, gentlemen, the meaning of the Greek word which expresses this special prerogative of man over the feeble intelligence of the inferior animals. It is called Logos: What does Logos mean? It stands both for *reason* and for *speech*, and it is difficult to say which it means more properly. It means both at once: Why? because really they cannot be divided,—because they are, in a true sense, one. When we can separate light and illumination, life and motion, the convex and the concave of a curve, then will it be possible for thought to tread speech under foot, and to hope to do without it—then will it be conceivable that the vigorous and fertile intellect should renounce its own double, its instrument of expression, and the channel of its speculations and emotions ".

SEAN O'CASEY

by DENIS JOHNSTONE

SEAN O'CASEY, as a writer, is not merely alive, he's kicking. His work, as one contemplates it, has all the static consistency of a volcano. The same smoke and violence—the same sense of a magnificent piece of natural self-expression that should be put to some useful purpose. And at the same time one feels a certain apprehension in approaching close enough to make this survey.

Yet it all began in such a bright and amusing way. About 1923, as far as I remember, the Abbey Theatre in Dublin billed a new play by a new Author, called " The Shadow of a Gunman ". It all takes place in a back room in a tenement house in Hilljoy Square, where a young poet is living—not a very good poet, I'm afraid,—and his principal interest to the other residents lies in the fact that they all suspect him of being a member of the Irish Republican Army on the run :—

MRS. HENDERSON : *Come along in, Mr. Gallicker. Mr. Davoran won't mind ; it's him as can put you in the way o' having your wrongs righted. Come on in, man, and don't be shy. Mr. Davoran is wan ov ourselves that stands for governmint ov the people with the people by the people. You must know in all fairity, Mr. Davoran, that the family livin' in the next room to Mr. Gallicker—the back drawin' room, to be particular—am I right or am I wrong, Mr. Gallicker ?*

MR. GALLOGHER : *You're right, Mrs. Henderson, perfectly right—that's the very identical room.*

MRS. HENDERSON : *Well, Mr. Davoran, the people in the back drawin' room, or to be more particular, the residents— that's the word that's writ in the letter—am I right or am I wrong, Mr. Gallicker ?*

MR. GALLOGHER : *You're right, Mrs. Henderson, perfectly accurate—that's the very identical word.*

MRS. HENDERSON : *Well, Mr. Davoran, the residents in the back drawin' room, as I aforesaid, is nothin' but a gang o' tramps that oughtn't to be allowed to associate with honest, decent, quiet, respectable people. Mr. Gallicker has tried to reason with them, and make them behave themselves—which in my opinion they never will—however, that's only an opinion, and not legal—ever since they have made Mr. Gallicker's life a HELL. Mr. Gallicker, am I right or am I wrong ?*

MR. GALLOGHER : *I'm sorry to say you're right, Mrs. Henderson, perfectly right—not a word of exaggeration.*

MRS. HENDERSON : *Well, now, Mr. Gallicker, seein' as I have given Mr. Davoran a fair account of how you're situated, an' of these tramps' cleverality, I'll ask you to read the letter which I'll say, not because you're there or that you're a friend of mine, is as good a letter as was decomposed by a scholar.*

We have quoted you this piece out of " The Gunman " because the play is not as well known as either " Juno " or " The Plough and the Stars " that followed it, and because you will see in it most of the things that made O'Casey's name famous at the start—his apparently sardonic sense of humour, his use of repeated phrases to

give a comic effect and an illusion of character, his
Dublinese vocabulary that you find in words like "cleverality". This play, followed by "Juno and the Paycock",
provided O'Casey with his first set of labels.

We are always putting critical labels on to people, and
O'Casey was a humourist, even though he called both
his plays "Tragedies". This, we thought, was probably
his most subtle joke of all. But even more certain, he was
a great Realist, writing with photographic accuracy
about the Dublin slums, in much the same way as an
earlier school of dramatists had drawn the life of the
Irish countryside.

Then came "The Plough", which looked superficially
as if it was intended to be a realistic play too. There was
the same broad comedy—the same slum vocabulary,—
the same catch phrases ; "Oh, that's a very derogatory
thing". But—well, listen to this :—

MRS. GOGAN : *Take your rovin' lumps of hands from
pattin' the bassinette, if you please ma'am ; an', steppin' from
the threshold of good manners, let me tell you, Mrs. Burgess,
that it's a fat wonder to Jennie Gogan that a lady-like singer
o' hymns like yourself would lower her thoughts from sky-
thinkin' to stretch out her arms in a sly-seekin' way to pinch
anything driven astray in the confusion of the battle our boys
is makin' for the freedom of their country.*
PETER : *Hee, hee, hee, hee ! I'll go with the pair of youse
an' give youse a hand.*
BESSIE : *Poverty an' hardship has sent Bessie Burgess to
abide with strange company, but she always knew them she
had to live with from backside to breakfast time ; an' she can
tell them always havin' had a Christian kinch on her conscience, that a passion for thievin' an' pinchin' would find her
soul a foreign place to live in, an' that her present intention is*

quite the lofty hearted one of pickin' up anything shaken up an'
scattered about in the loose confusion of a general plunder.

That is eloquence all right, but by no manner of means
could it ever be described as realism. So O'Casey
promptly had to be clothed with a slightly different
garment—the mantle of J. M. Synge was the nearest
thing. Like Synge he was supposed to be a poet writing
prose—an Olympian observer, looking down with a
certain detached amusement on the struggles of the people
he was writing about—taking no sides—grinding no axes.
He was also a Pacifist and a debunker of nationalism and
all that sort of thing; and in this guise he was delivered by
his native City to London, where he came under the
attention of an even Higher Criticism, and the confusion
in due course became even worse confounded.

Because, mark this well ; from 1927 onwards, O'Casey
started writing plays that fitted in with no preconceived
notion of the kind of man we had decided him to be.
They were partisan, they were bitter, they were full of
imagery and verse and symbolism that were the last
things that you would expect from a slum realist. Many
people adored them.

Let's make no mistake about that. Indeed, T. E.
Lawrence and the Shaws went so far as to say that the
second Act of the " Silver Tassie "—the War Act—was
the finest thing that had been written for the stage in the
English language. You may remember, for example, the
prayer of the soldiers to the big gun :—

> " *Hail, cool-hardened tower of steel embossed*
> *With the fevered figment thoughts of man ;*
> *Guardian of our love and hate and fear*
> *Speak for us to the inner ear of God.*
> *We believe in God and we believe in thee.*

Jailed in thy steel are hours of merriment
Cadged from the pageant-dream of children's play
Too soon of the motley stripped that they may sweat
With them that toil for the glory of thy kingdom.

We believe in God and we believe in thee ".

But this high opinion of the " Tassie " wasn't every-body's view. This wasn't the kind of play that was expected of O'Casey, and to begin with, it was turned down by the Abbey Theatre—an act of considerable courage on Yeat's part, if I may say so. It took O'Casey a very long time to get over this treatment of his play, because he is not the kind of man to take dictation from anybody on the kind of play he ought to write. And ever since then he has gone on writing plays in the same style, and I have no doubt whatever that he will continue to do so, in spite of all the wringing of Irish hands over the lost Author of " Juno ". Indeed, I scarcely like to think what Dublin must be saying about his last play— " Oakleaves and Lavender ". For the Pacifist and the anti-nationalist, who wrote the " Silver Tassie ", Mr. O'Casey, through his character Drishogue, goes consider-ably further than most Englishmen would dare, in stating " For What we Fight " :—

" *For the greatness of England's mighty human soul set forth in what Shakespeare, Keats and Milton sang ; for the mighty compass of Darwin's mind, sweeping back to the beginning and forward to the end ; for what your Faraday did in taming the lightning to stream quietly about in the service of man ; and if these be indifferent things to you, then fight and die, if need be, in the halo of healing from the tiny light carried in the lovely delicate hands of Florence Nightingale. Go forth and fight, perchance to die, for the great human soul of England. In this*

*fight, Edgar, righteousness and war have kissed each other ;
Christ, Mahomet, Confucius and Buddha are one ".*

How's that for the ex-Secretary of the Irish Citizen
Army ? At this point, I think, we may safely throw
overboard the last of our preconceived notions about
Sean O'Casey, and reconcile ourselves to the fact that
there must be something wrong with the data. It is
obvious that he's not just being " contrary "—he is not
just being " cussed " because Yeats rejected the " Tassie ".
The answer, of course, lies in the kind of man O'Casey
is himself, and if we don't get that right at the outset we
are going to experience a lot of difficulty in talking about
his plays at all.

If you have seen the recent production of " Red Roses
for Me " you may have been a little puzzled—as I was—
by the fact that the officer representing the Dublin
Metropolitan Police in this drama of the Great Dublin
Strike of 1913 wears a magnificent red plume in his
helmet. Now in my recollection of the D.M.P. at this
period, they never wore any plumes in their helmets, red
or otherwise. And if they had tried to do so, the laugh
they would have raised in the Dublin streets would have
been nobody's business ! When I asked O'Casey about
this, thinking perhaps that his recollection might be at
fault, he answered quite blandly that he knew that the
D.M.P. did not wear plumes, but that he liked a bit of
colour, and that the thing symbolised the man's virility.

Now there you have the beginning of the real O'Casey,
and if you cling on to that, and don't get misled by things
in his first two plays, you will find a certain consistency
in all his work—a consistency that runs right through
from his first book, " The Story of the Irish Citizen
Army " to " Oakleaves and Lavender ". He likes a bit

of colour. In other words, he isn't a realist at all, and
never regarded himself as one.

O'Casey, for all his reputation, is actually a dyed-in-
the-wool Romantic, living in a world of heroes and
villains, with a deep and sincere regard for Poetry and
Colour. He is sincere because he is no fool with regard
to either poetry or colour. People have been known to
say that O'Casey " kids himself " that he is a Poet, but
this isn't so at all. For all his colourful writing and his
lavish use of adjectives, O'Casey does not profess to be a
Poet, and if you ask him what he would really like to
have been, he will probably answer—like Shaw—a
Painter.

But when I say that he is no fool and knows his own
limitations, I don't want to deny the existence of those
limitations. To my mind at any rate, there is a certain
indiscipline—maybe a certain naivetie, in his taste. On
one side of his study you will find Giorgione's " Sleeping
Venus "—the picture that features in the first Act of " The
Plough ". And facing it is a Gaugin reproduction.
Now apart from the fact that they both begin with a G,
there is not much in common between Giorgione and
Gaugin, and although this may be a point in favour of the
Catholicity of O'Casey's mind, the fact that he should
choose to sit in his holy of holies enjoying both of them
simultaneously suggests to me that—although he undoubtedly knows what he likes—possibly he doesn't
quite know Why.

It seems to me to be precisely this that induces him to
put a red plume on the helmet of a member of the
Dublin Metropolitan Police. He likes a bit of colour,
and in his heart of hearts he thinks that his Joxers and his
Paycocks and his Fluthers—the children of his brain that
have made his reputation and endeared him to us in

" Juno " and " The Plough and the Stars "—are really rather drab characters, and that he ought to do better than that.

It is just the same with his prose. The bareness of nouns should be embellished with adjectives, and the ungrammatical reality of speech should be given a rhythm and a bit of decoration, as Shakespeare did in his time. In his early plays you get him feeling tentatively after this. " Juno " has its off-stage chorus of " Coal blocks. Coal blocks ". And in " The Plough " we hear the chanting of " Ambulance. Ambulance. Red Cross. Ambulance ". The drunken Fluther beats out a rhythm on the door of the tenement as he tries to get in with a barrel of beer on his shoulder.

" *Get us a mug or a jug or somethin', some o' youse, one o' youse, will youse, before I lay one o' youse out. Come down an' open the door, some o' youse, one o' youse, will youse, before I lay one o' youse out* ".

But this isn't good enough for O'Casey. This is only a start—a try-out. In these first three plays, which now frankly bore him, he is only feeling his way towards a fuller and much more elaborate technique that is to come later on. If they appear to be realistic to us, that is only because he is a beginner.

And in just the same way, if he appears to be detached and undogmatic in his sentiments or in his attitude towards his characters, this is not because he is himself a neutral. He is keeping what he wants to say until he feels that he can say it in the way that he likes.

That is why it is all wrong to regard O'Casey as a brilliant artist who has lost his way after three successful plays. There is a steady and deliberate thread running through all his work, and if Sean O'Casey has gone the

way he has gone, it is not because he couldn't write
another " Juno ", but because he no longer likes that kind
of play. If you happen to like it better than " The Star
Turns Red ", that's just too bad for you and me.

Which brings me to my next point about the real
O'Casey. He is a man of enormous integrity and of
great seriousness. Neither his pen nor his name are for
sale, which is probably why he never went to Hollywood
as he could easily have done, in the past. We may agree
or disagree with his views on politics and on what constitutes good Theatre, but he will not change them or
temper them to the needs of the Box Office. He writes
that way because he likes it that way, and there is no use
our telling him how we would write his plays, because
he has something to say, and say it he will in his own
way, whether we like it or not. If we choose to regard
his declared Tragedies as roaring Comedies that doesn't
make him a Humourist.

So much for what he thinks about it. On our own
part, I think we may fairly retort to Mr. O'Casey that
the style of writing that he is so deliberately adopting is
not so much a development of " The Plough and the
Stars " as a return to his earlier technique. Maybe he
intends to come full circle ; or maybe he intends to go
further back still to something Elizabethan. Here, as an
example, is the way in which he began writing. In his
first book, " The Story of the Irish Citizen Army " he
is describing a Labour meeting at which Jim Larkin is
about to appear, and he does it in this way.

" *The disappearing Artist Sun had boldly brushed the skies
with bold hues of orange and crimson, and delicate shades of
yellow and green, bordered with dusky shadows of darkening
blue, which seemed to symbolise the glow of determination, the*

delicate hues of hope, and the bordering shades of restless anxiety that coloured the hearts and thoughts of the waiting, watching masses of men that stood silently beneath the oriental-coloured panoply of the sky ".

I am sure you will agree with me that even in those days Sean O'Casey liked a bit of colour. But let us now compare it to this.

" *The December sun had hidden its dull rays behind the huge rocks that rose monstrously west of Dunfern Mansion, and ceased to gladden the superb apartment Sir John occupied most of the day.*

" *Viewing the dazzling glow of splendour which shone through spectacles of wonder in all its glory, Sir John felt his past life but a dismal dream, brightened here and there with a crystal speck of sunshine that had partly hidden its gladdening rays of bright futurity until compelled to glitter with the daring effect they should produce ".*

That last—tell it not in Gath—is by another Elizabethan born out of time, the late Mrs. Amanda McKittric Ros. And when I say it is " Elizabethan ", I do not mean that it is Shakespearean. I am referring to that early school of decorative writers known as the Euphuists.

Now maybe this is a little unfair, to dig up Mr. O'Casey's first book. But after all, what about his latest, where an Air Force Cadet is expected to say :

" *Our spring will still have many a frosty morning and a frosty night ; our summers hot hold many a burden for us ; our autumn glory will still be tinged with many a starless night, the sound of sorrow loud beneath their shrouded silence ; but winter's night of hopeless woe is gone for ever, and the people's energetic joy shall sound like well-cast bells through every passing season ".*

Heaven forbid that I should set myself up as a critic. What to one writer is poetry, to another writer is a wilderness of words, and maybe the popular taste for the rococo will come back.

But for the present, I personally prefer the more direct, if gloomier statement : " The whole world's in a terrible state of chassis ".

Not so, O'Casey.   Like Halley's Comet he has quite deliberately gone off on an orbit of his own ; and Professor Einstein has taught us that it is useless to speculate whether he has left us or we have left him.   Suffice to say, if we wait long enough, like Halley's Comet he will probably complete his course in his own time, and come back again.

Meanwhile, we may well ask—" What is the stars ? Joxer.   What is the stars ? "

GRAHAM GREENE

by ARTHUR CALDER-MARSHALL

ENGLISH LITERATURE in the inter-war years falls into two periods ; the post-war period and the post-depression period. The post-war period was one of dis-enchantment. The Edwardian world had gone ; values were shattered ; moral and political ideas succumbed to the economic attacks of Marx and Lenin, the psychological attack of Freud and Jung. " The Waste Land " was the battlefield of Flanders extended to the fields of post-war conduct, ethics and social theory, a sort of mopping-up operation, clearing aside beliefs, slaughtered in the course of the war.

In their place, were set few positive beliefs ; and certainly none which were universally accepted. So, the writer of the thirties, the post-depression writer could take little for granted. He was like a dramatist, who besides writing his play, must build his theatre and con-struct his scenery. The beliefs which, for example, Dickens or Thackeray, or even the fathers of the intellect-ual revolution, Wells and Shaw, could take for granted, had all gone by the board. The only two certainties of the thirties were economic insecurity and the threat of war. " Who live under the shadow of a war, what can

we do that matters ? " asked Stephen Spender. The
shadow of war, for Eliot, Graves, Sassoon, meant
1914-18. But for Spender and his generation, it meant
—the war to come.

Of the English novelists of the Thirties, none in my
opinion, was more accomplished or more sensitive to the
spirit of his time, than Graham Greene. " Spirit " is
probably the wrong word. The shape, the pattern, the
conflict of spiritual forces was caught infinitely better by
Rex Warner, in " The Wild Goose Chase ", " The
Professor " and " The Aerodrome ". But the feel and
the smell of the Thirties was caught by Greene—especially
the smell. Rex Warner diagnosed the disease : Graham
Greene analysed the symptoms with loving care.

The disenchantment of the Twenties—a matter of the
mind and the emotions—became in the Thirties, even
more a matter of economics, politics and war, a matter
of life and death. For D. H. Lawrence in the Twenties,
there was still the mysticism of the dark pulse of the
blood. For Greene and others in the Thirties, there was
the gathering of evil and violence, from Manchuria,
Abyssinia, Spain, the shadows cast by war came closer
home and closer ; and every year, the mounting frustra-
tion, indignity and disgust.

Contemporary novelists, like Elizabeth Bowen, were
content to sketch the background, just enough to make
their characters indentifiable. But Graham Greene lifted
his ideas direct from contemporary newspapers. The
financial juggling of Ivar Krogh in " England Made Me "
was suggested by the suicide of Kreuger, the Swedish
Match King : " Brighton Rock " sprang from the
Brighton Race Gang Murders ; " Confidential Agent "
derived from the Spanish Civil War ; " The Power and
the Glory " from Garrido's anti-clerical governorship of
Tabasco in Mexico.

As with ideas, for plots, so with characters : Minty, the miserable expatriate anglo-catholic old Harrovian ; Tony Farrant, the attractive public school man, a failure in a dozen capitals ; Surrogate, the weak, sensual, wealthy " Leftist " ; Pinky Brown, the strange criminal product of Brighton slum-life and of a certain type of Roman Catholicism ; eternal types maybe, but clothed in the fashions of the thirties. Even the locations, the incidents, are taken from everyday life, the topical life of the thirties. The source-material for Greene's novels, in fact, might have been the " Police Gazette ", " The News of the World", and the files of "Mass Observation".

But that doesn't mean that Graham Greene is a mere reporter. In fact, he is not an accurate reporter, nor is he interested in being one. Contemporary life provides the symbols he needs. In the old-fashioned sense, there is no " comment " ; no appeals to the " dear reader ". The novel appears straight, fast, factual narrative with a concentration on objective detail. Here for example, in " England Made Me ", is Minty, the seedy journalist, getting up in the morning :—

" *Minty knew the moment that he got up in the morning that this was one of his days. He sang gently to himself as he shaved, ' This is the way that Minty goes, Minty goes, Minty goes ". Although he had a new blade he did not cut himself once ; he shaved cautiously rather than closely, while the pot of coffee, which his landlady had brought him, grew cold on the washstand. Minty liked his coffee cold ; his stomach would bear nothing hot. A spider watched him under his tooth-glass ; it had been there five days ; he had expected his landlady to clear it away, but it had remained a second day, a third day. She must believe that he kept it there for study. He wondered how long it would live. He watched it, and it watched him back with shaggy patience. It had lost a leg when he put the glass over it.*

"*Above his bed was a house group, rows of boys blinking against the sun above and below the seated figures of the prefects, the central figure of the housemaster and his wife.*

"*It was curious to observe how a moustache by being waxed at the tips could date a man as accurately as a woman's dress, white blouse, the whalebone collar, the puffed sleeves. Occasionally Minty was called on to identify himself; practice had made him perfect; there had been a time of hesitation when he could not decide whether Patterson seated on the housemaster's left or Tester standing rather more obscurely behind, his jaw hidden by a puffed sleeve, best acted as his proxy. For Minty himself did not appear; he had seen the photograph taken from the sickroom window, a blaze of light, the blinking blackened faces, the photographer diving beneath his shade.*

"'*This is the way that Minty goes*'. *He picked a stump of cigarette from the soap tray and lit it. Then he studied his hair in the mirror of the wardrobe door; this was one of his days; he must be prepared for anything, even society. The scurf worried him; he rubbed what was left of the pomade upon his scalp, brushing his hair, studied it again. Minty was satisfied. He drank his tepid coffee without taking the cigarette from his mouth; the smoke blew up and burned his eyes. He swore so gently that no one but himself would have known he swore. 'Holy Cnut'. The phrase was his own; always, instinctively, like a good Anglo-catholic, he disliked 'smut'; it was as satisfying to say 'Holy Cnut' as words that sullied*".

That is typical Graham Greene. Superficially, Minty is just getting up in the morning. But there is a lot more to it than that. Greene has introduced almost all the threads from which he weaves Minty's character. His Anglo-catholicism, his Harrow fixation, his seediness, his operation, the cold coffee, the desire to torture others in order to relieve his own misery—to play with the spider under the glass as God plays with him. From these fragments Minty is built up ; variations and developments of these elements give him life. But as well as life, Minty has a purpose, a philosophical role to play in the development of the novel ; and that purpose is enunciated between a semicolon and a full stop. " He must be prepared for anything, even society ". The theme of " England Made Me ", as of every book which Greene has written, is the relation of man to society ; with the individual as the victim, and society the villain ; and it is in the theme, more than in any of the characters, that the author is interested.

In 1936, Greene published a book called "Journey without Maps ". It is an account of a most terrifying journey into the interior—the interior being the interior of Graham Greene. It is a fascinating book, which unfortunately had to be withdrawn. Greene, describing some peculiarly seedy character he had met, realised that he must disguise the character with a false name, and dipping into his unconscious for the most unlikely name, happened to choose the name of one of the most respected citizens of Sierra Leone, who promptly took legal action.

I am glad to say, though, that " Journey without Maps" is going to be republished shortly. In it Greene is at his most self-revealing. And his attitude to characters like Minty in his novels is made clear when he talks about " that odd assortment of ' characters ' one collects through life, vivid grotesques, people so simple that they always have the same side turned to one, damned by their unselfconsciousness to be material for the novelist, to supply the minor characters, to be endlessly caricatured, to make in their multiplicity one's world ".

These are the minor characters, the vivid grotesques ; Conder, the journalist in " It's a Battlefield ", living over a Soho cafe, collecting foreign coins, but with a dozen fantasy lives—the invented wife and family, the innumerable domestic worries existing only in imagination. What one may call major characters are slightly more developed—the whiskey priest in " The Power and the Glory ", or Pinky in " Brighton Rock ". And who would it be in " It's a Battlefield ? "—Conrad Drover perhaps . . .

They are none of them really major characters, though, so much as central characters. With all the others they make, in their multiplicity, Graham Greene's world. But they always remain subservient to the pattern, the theme, the argument of the author ; they never get out of hand, as for example, Mr. Micawber so frequently does in " David Copperfield ". Greene creates his characters for a purpose and holds them to it.

And that purpose is to express his own philosophy. What the philosophy is, it is impossible to extract from the novels ; because it *is* the novels. But there are certain elements which Greene detects in himself. He admits to the conflicting tendencies, firstly to expect things to be better than they are, and secondly to suspect when things appear to be better when they're really worse. In his approach to people and to society, he is a pessimist. His Catholic hero-villain, the unspeakable Pinky Brown, believes in one Devil. " Credo in unum Satanum ". Greene's own conviction of evil preceded his belief in God. In " The Lawless Roads ", he writes :—

" *And so faith came to one—shapelessly, without dogma, a presence above a croquet lawn, something associated with*

violence, cruelty, evil across the way. One began to believe
in heaven, because one believed in hell, but for a long while it
was hell only one could picture with a certain intimacy—the
pitch-pine partitions in dormitories where everybody was never
quiet at the same time : lavatories without locks—' There, by
the reason of the great number of the damned, the prisoners
are heaped together in their awful prison . . .' walks in
pairs up the metroland road, no solitude anywhere, at any
time. The Anglican Church could not supply the same
intimate symbols for heaven ; only a big brass eagle, an organ
voluntary, ' Lord dismiss us with Thy blessing ', the quiet
croquet lawn where one had no business, the rabbit and the
distant music."

It is this conviction of evil which gives to his work
its intensity. The prose carefully free from direct
comment, is vivid with comment metaphors, which
build up the atmosphere of horror, disgust, evil, terror,
loneliness.

" The moonlight through the unprotected glass made them
into blue cold shabby squares *like the* used ice *at fishmongers'*.
In one room she found in a grate a ball of hair combings as
large as a baby's skull* *and on the floor in another room an
unreceipted bill for a pair of corsets. She made her way to the
top, to the two rooms where there was only a smell of stale air
and a dead bat on the floor, like a bundle of brown knitting ".

Here is another " comment metaphor ", which is
rather more carefully worked out :—

" The room was full of women, their faces old and unlined
and pencilled in brilliant colours, like the illumination of an
ancient missal carefully preserved under glass with the same
page always turned to visitors ".

* *The emphasis is Mr. Calder-Marshall's.*

That is from " England Made Me ", and here is another from " The Power and the Glory " :—

" *Mr. Tench's father had been a dentist too—his first memory was finding a discarded cast in a wastepaper basket— the rough toothless gaping mouth of clay, like something dug up in Dorset—Neanderthal or Pithecanthropus. It had been his favourite toy : they tried to tempt him with Meccano : but fate had struck.*

" *There is always one moment in childhood when the door opens and lets the future in. The hot, wet river-port and the vultures lay in the waste-paper basket. We should be thankful we cannot see the horrors and degradations lying around our childhood, in cupboards and bookshelves, everywhere* ".

For those who are Roman Catholics, a gleam of hope emerges in Greene's later work, notably in " The Power and the Glory ", in which the priest says :—

" *We've always said the poor are blessed and the rich are going to find it hard to get into heaven. Why should we make it hard for the poor man too ? Oh, I know we are told to give to the poor, to see they are not hungry—hunger can make a man do evil just as much as money can. But why should we give the poor power ? It's better to let him die in dirt and wake in heaven—so long as we don't push his face in the dirt* ".

" Why should we give the poor power ? " the priest says. In the world I see emerging, the poor after having their faces pushed in the dirt are not being given power ; they are taking it. And for one I say " Good Luck to them ". I personally find that remark of the " whisky priest ", or the faith of Pinky Brown more horrible and terrifying than balls of hair combings as large as babies' skulls.

But it does not diminish my admiration for him as a writer. All art is partial. The decade of the thirties was one of transition, in which the old world of class privilege was already dying, and in which the believers in a new socialist society were growing up. Greene seized on the dying points, the lumpen elements of every class ; and from them he created his vivid grotesques of the old society in its death throes. He was right, because it was those dying elements which were dragging the world, and being dragged themselves to disaster. Minty and Farrant, Pinky Brown and Rose ; those were the marginal types, the first casualties because the most exposed. To Greene, or perhaps it is to his whisky priest, Britain has now entered a new phase of horror ; the one in which the poor have power ; (but in which of course the former rich will find it easier to enter Heaven). It will be interesting to see if the defeated and seedy types of the forties and fifties will be as significant as they were in the thirties.

CHRISTOPHER ISHERWOOD

by W. J. TURNER

THE FIRST BOOK I read by Christopher Isherwood was "Sally Bowles", published in 1937. It was probably written earlier than "Mr. Norris Changes Trains", which was published in 1935. I am speaking from internal evidence for I have not yet succumbed to that form of dreariness which looks up dates and inflicts an audience with facts which they could look up for themselves. So I hope that straightway I have provided you with something interesting to do—which is to make enquiries for yourselves.

Christopher Isherwood may not be a great writer—there are very few of them in any century—but at least he is a real writer and not a pretentious bore ; or not yet.

Intelligent reviewers, and those who like to pass for critics, would probably consider him to be a sort of minor and inferior Aldous Huxley, but I would protest that he is more human than Huxley, far more human, and slightly less concerned with his own soul. It is his humanity which appeals to me, and there is the additional fact that he makes me laugh. And not occasionally, but often and loudly. Recently I thought I had better read him again to make sure whether he could make me laugh a second time. For that is the real test. Not that I find it easy to laugh. Many of you do find it easy, perhaps ? If so, I envy you. It has been my fate to go to music-halls and revues very often and never to laugh once. I have listened to world famous comedians and during a whole evening I have only produced one faintly grim smile.

It is necessary for me to tell you this so that you should know that it means something when I say Isherwood makes me laugh ; and, especially, when I add that on re-reading " Sally Bowles " I laughed just as much although the novelty had worn off.

" Sally Bowles " remains a *creation*, done in one hundred and fifty very short pages. Most of our famous living novelists fail to create anyone in three hundred and fifty very *long* pages. But then, they are either too solemn and pretentious or too conventional and obvious. Most artists who fail, fail because they are neither modest nor simple enough to be themselves. Isherwood is both modest and simple, although he thinks himself to be very complicated, and so he is interested in what happens to him. And he is not afraid to let it happen. If very little that is interesting happens to most of us, it is chiefly because we are always frightened of what we may be letting ourselves in for. We sheer off out of our instinct for self-preservation. Now I shall not hide from you my opinion that the real Sally Bowles must have been a frightful bore. Personally I couldn't have stood her for five minutes, but Isherwood did, and here I should add that I am sure he drew her (as all novelists draw their best characters) from life. He gave himself up to this experience out of his own receptive sympathy, and it is his own sensitive sympathy and understanding—so individual and full of flavour—which creates Sally Bowles and makes her story slight as it is, a real living book and

D

not one hundred and fifty pages of dead words.

But Isherwood has done more than make Sally Bowles
live. He has also made her representative, he has created
a type. To show this I must make a quotation.

She rings up Isherwood one day, asking him to come
and see her at once. When he arrives, the following
dialogue, which I shall cut a little, takes place :

" ' *Do you want to earn some money, darling ?* '

" ' *Of course* '.

" ' *Splendid !   You see it's like this . . .* '

" *She was in a fluffy pink dressing-wrap and inclined to be
breathless :*

" ' *There's a man I know who's starting a magazine.   It's
going to be most terribly highbrow and artistic, with lots of
marvellous modern photographs . . . you know the sort of
thing . . . Well, the first country they're going to do is
England and they want me to write an article on the English
Girl.   Of course I haven't the foggiest idea what to say, so
what I thought was : you could write the article in my name,
and get the money—I only want not to disoblige this man
who's editing the paper because he may be terribly useful to me
in other ways, later on . . .* '

" ' *All right, I'll try* '.

" ' *Oh, marvellous !* '

" ' *How soon do you want it done ?* '

" ' *You see, darling, that's the whole point.   I must have
it at once . . . otherwise it's no earthly use, because I promised
it four days ago, and I simply must have it this evening . . .
It needn't be very long.   About five hundred words* '.

" ' *Well, I'll do my best* '.

" ' *Good, that's wonderful . . . Sit down wherever you
like.   Here's some paper.   You've got a pen ?   Oh, and here's
a dictionary, in case there's a word you can't spell . . . I'll
just be having my bath* '.

" When, three-quarters of an hour later, Sally came in dressed for the day, I had finished. Frankly I was rather pleased with my effort.

" She read it through carefully, a slow frown gathering between her beautifully pencilled eyebrows. When she had finished she laid down the manuscript with a sigh.

" ' I'm sorry, Chris, it won't do at all '.

" ' Won't do ? ' I was genuinely taken aback.

" ' Of course, I dare say it's very good from a literary point of view, and all that . . .'

" ' Well, then, what's wrong with it ? '

" ' It's not nearly snappy enough'. Sally was final.

" ' It's not the kind of thing this man wants at all '.

" I shrugged my shoulders . . . There was a resentful pause.

" ' My goodness, I know who'll do it for me if I ask him ! ' cried Sally, suddenly jumping up. ' Why on earth didn't I think of him before ? ' She grabbed the telephone and dialled a number.

" ' Oh, hello, Kurt, darling . . .' In three minutes she had explained all about the article.

" Replacing the receiver . . . she announced triumphantly :

" ' That's marvellous ! He's going to do it at once . . .'

" She paused impressively and added :

" ' That was Kurt Rosenthal '.

" ' Who's he ? '

" ' You've never heard of him ? '

" This annoyed Sally. ' I thought you took an interest in the cinema ? He's miles the best young scenario-writer. He earns pots of money. He's only doing this as a favour to me, of course. He says he'll dictate it to his secretary while shaving . . . . That's the sort of writer I admire . . . he can write anything—anything you like : scenarios, novels, plays, poetry, advertisements . . .'

" *Irritated as I was with her, I couldn't help laughing* ".

Well, there's the Sally Bowles who is typical of
hundreds of thousands of young women in England and
America today. Here she is, I won't say fully, but livingly
presented and whereas you, perhaps, and certainly I,
would have found her too disgusting to spend five
minutes in her company, Mr. Isherwood, though injured
and irritated by her, can do her more than justice, can
give her life on the printed page. Perhaps you think this
is easy. Well, think of anyone you know, and try it !
Then if you succeed in writing a single page of living
dialogue, look up the scene Mr. Isherwood has written of
her visit to the German Police. Not only will it make
you laugh aloud but it will fill you with delicious envy
if you are capable of appreciating brilliant writing.
Perhaps " Mr. Norris Changes Trains " is an even better
book ; it is certainly a fuller and more detailed portrait.
And it shows Mr. Isherwood in his full humanity.

Nothing in human nature comes amiss to him, so wide
and rich is his sympathy ; but he is as critical as he is
sympathetic ; it is the combination of extreme intelligence and warm sympathy that makes his writing
remarkable in its freedom from cant, conventionality
and hypocritical moral judgments.

In " Lions and Shadows ", published in 1937, Mr.
Isherwood gives an enlightening ,vivid sketch of himself.

" *I was* " he says, " *a born film fan . . . inside a cinema
I seemed to lose all critical sense* ".

He goes on to say that if he went to a cinema with a
friend he was " *perpetually on the defensive, excusing the
film's absurdities, eagerly praising its slightest merits* " ; and
he then explains—" *the reason for this had, I think, very*

little to do with Art . . . I was, and still am, endlessly interested in the outward appearance of people—their facial expressions, their gestures, their walk, their nervous tricks, their infinitely various ways of eating a sausage, opening a paper parcel, lighting a cigarette. The cinema puts people under a microscope : you can stare at them, you can examine them as though they were insects. True, the behaviour you see on the screen isn't natural behaviour ; it is acting and often very bad acting. But the acting has always a certain relation to ordinary life ; and after a short while, to an habitué like myself, it is as little of an annoyance as Elizabethan handwriting is to the expert in old documents . . ."

There is a lot more I could say about Mr. Isherwood (who I may add is personally unknown to me) if I had the space. I must therefore restrict myself to emphasising the fact that I think him the best comic writer—apart from Evelyn Waugh—living today.

But comic writers rarely develop, I am grieved to say. Is there any development in Tchekhov or in W. S. Gilbert—I name two of the most brilliant comic writers ? When they are good, they are simply marvellous. You can read them again and again for they are, like Shakespeare, profoundly wise. But if they do not develop it is because, unlike Shakespeare, they have no " Bottom " to their wisdom ; they do not go deep enough to speak from some immovable foundation in themselves which is not a conventional foundation. Mr. Isherwood is young and may yet prove an exception. His last book, "Prater Violet", which most reviewers saw as revealing nothing new, gave me a different impression. I thought it showed development ; there was in it an indication of a sense of pure values—chiefly in the sympathetic portrait of the film-director, Bergman.

It is notorious that all novelists fail when trying to
portray a great man. Well, Mr. Isherwood has succeeded. His Bergman is a truly great man and, so far,
nobody has noticed it. He is great because he represents
a supremely high spiritual value, that is real and not a
sham. Most of Mr. Isherwood's people are very far from
being great, but he is just to them, partly I think because
his sense of value is so acute and so sound, as he reveals
incidentally in his portrait of the violinist Cheuret in
" Lions and Shadows ". For the writer who could
portray Cheuret and Bergman as well as Sally Bowles
and Mr. Norris, there is indeed hope. In the meantime,
I must express my personal gratitude to the brilliant
comic genius who wrote the passage in " Lions and
Shadows " about " the Mud-Coloured File ". I have
laughed more profoundly over that than over anything
else outside the very best of Tchekhov. There is very
little pure humour in the world, but it is here.

" *Letters and copies of answers had, of course, to be filed.
We had bought a very handsome file dull grey in colour, which
opened like a concertina—it was known, always, as ' The
Mud-Coloured File '.*

" *This file gave me more trouble than any other inanimate
object I have ever encountered, before or since. How often,
on arrival, I would be greeted by Rose or Jean or Edward from
the top of the staircase with the news : ' The Mud-Coloured
File's lost again ! Have you seen it ? The Governor's been
hunting for hours ! ' And then, at last, it would be discovered,
lying innocently unnoticed on a chair, toning perfectly with the
dull grey shadows of a late autumn morning and, from the
distance of a few yards, nearly invisible. Not only could the
mud-coloured file uncannily disappear ; its roomy pockets
seemed to swallow litter like a conjuror's vanishing box.*

*Cheuret's conception of filing differs radically from my own :
if he put a paper away under the letter P, then I was sure to
hunt for it in M, N, O, Q and R—and vice versa. At last
by mutual consent we stopped using the file altogether; except
for correspondence which was no longer important. Urgent
letters were popped into the suitcase, slipped between sheets of
music or left lying on the sitting-room mantlepiece, as in the
days before my arrival".*

I shall not say much about Isherwood's plays ; chiefly
because they were written in collaboration with W. H.
Auden. I saw both " The Dog Beneath the Skin " and
" The Ascent of F 6 " at the Westminster Theatre,
London, and was much disappointed in them, as I had
expected to find dramatic talent in Auden—about whom,
however, I am not here concerned. " The Dog Beneath
the Skin " was slightly better than " The Ascent of F 6,"
but they were both ruined by an obsession with half-
baked psycho-analytical theories.

If we like to amuse ourselves using the jargon of
psycho-analysis, we might affirm that creative writing—
unlike introspection—is an extrovert activity, and
although, as Jung has shown, there is hardly such a
person as a complete extrovert or a complete introvert ;
but that all of us are mixed (and not simply mixed
either)—yet in writing you must embody forth your
ideas and feelings, you have to give them form. That is
to say, you must *create*, and if as an introvert you first
look within, *then* you must next body forth what you
have found into outward shapes. I would not say it was
impossible to make a drama of abstractions, of ideas.
Shaw has done it, so has Shakespeare. But Shaw's
abstractions too often seem no more than vivid shadows
as against the suffering flesh and blood of Shakespeare's.

The Auden-Isherwood dramatic abstractions are not even vivid shadows, they are no more than snapshots out of propagandist scrap-books.

On the whole I like best of Mr. Isherwood's books the two described by him as works of fiction : " Sally Bowles " and " Mr. Norris Changes Trains ", for they are the purest Isherwood, the most individual and the most comical. But that remarkable character of his in " Prater Violet ", Mr. Bergman, spoke of another which was apparently the only one he had read, " The Memorial ". This novel Mr. Isherwood describes as a " Portrait of a Family ", and it is a very good one. Mr. Bergman called it " genial ", which is a word foreigners of Germanic speech use of any literary or musical composition they consider to show true creative talent, and my respect for Mr. Bergman is so great that I cannot think him wrong. " The Memorial " is undoubtedly a remarkable novel, owing something perhaps to E. M. Forster and Virginia Woolf. If I am not as enthusiastic about it as I am about " Sally Bowles " and " Mr. Norris Changes Trains " it is because I find some of the characters in it extremely tiresome, because not entirely real and convincing. Edward is a frightful bore, and the hero, Eric, who seems to be partly a self-portrait of Isherwood, is Isherwood without any of his talent or virtue.

Authors very very rarely do themselves justice when they try to draw a self-portrait. And, by the way, this applies to painters as well as to novelists. The reason is that they mistake what is important in themselves ; they know of their vices (of which they are terribly self-conscious) and are naturally quite unaware of their best qualities. Isherwood knows that he can write dialogue, but it seems to be the only thing he does know about himself. He seems quite unaware of his profound sense of humour, of his immense charity, and of his rare courage. That is what helps to make him so charming and it explains also why his heroes (Edward and Eric of " The Memorial "), because they are self-portraits, are such insufferable and boring nonentities, whilst his villains or rogues such as Sally and Mr. Norris, being true self-portraits, are simply delightful.

ELIZABETH BOWEN

by L. A. G. STRONG

SOMEONE WHOSE JUDGMENT I greatly respect,
on hearing that I was to talk about the work of Elizabeth
Bowen, said, " You're not at all the right person to do
that. You're an extraverted writer. You can't enter into
her ways of seeing things ". I sympathised with this
remark, because my critic loves Elizabeth Bowen's work.
It means a great deal to her : her way of experiencing
the world is not unlike the experience reflected in Elizabeth Bowen's writings : and so it was natural that she,
an introverted type, should feel she had a kind of private
understanding with these books, into which I could not
enter.

But while I sympathise with this view, I am not sure
that it is necessarily right. I am not sure that a writer of
one sort, in my case the sort that looks for truth outward
towards the object, may not have something useful to say
about the other sort, the sort that looks inward and
studies the reflection of the object on his or her own
personality. Not that Elizabeth Bowen is wholly that
sort of writer : but, if we are talking of those two sorts,
she is nearer to it than to the first—and that in spite
of an extraordinarily accurate observation of the details

of the external world. My point is that even if one happens to write in one way, one is not disqualified from appraising work done in a different way. So I shall regard the objection as a challenge rather than an axiom. No living writer interests me more than Elizabeth Bowen. I admire her work greatly, and I am writing about it of my own choice : so here goes.

She is an exceedingly difficult writer to classify. Let us leave aside all labels of objective and subjective, extravert and introvert, and note some of the details of her practice. First of all, she is an Irish writer—as Irish as Yeats. That means, among other things, that she is very strongly conscious of light. The Western landscape, whether in Ireland or in the West Highlands, derives its quality from the effects of light. This will at once strike anyone who has been dazzled by the sparkle of a road in Achill after rain. It is a physical fact, not merely an effect of magic on the beholder. A film company in Skye found all their previous experience of photography out of doors set at naught by the power, the variety, the ebullience of the light, even on an overcast day. And this phenomenon, this emanation from their inconstant skies, this elusive visitant that gives their scene its colour and its spirit, haunts from their earliest years the consciousness of Irish writers.

It teaches a purely visual artist such as Liam O'Flaherty to project his figures with stereoscopic clearness, splashed with wet light against a background of lowering mountain and their own dark, vivid shadows. It encourages the more indrawn Daniel Corkery to surround the heads of his people with a luminous aura, causing saint and sinner to shine in a bemused radiance. The characters of Sean O'Faolain can seize on it and wrap themselves in a shining cloak which sometimes hinders our vision of

them. Peadar O'Donnell sees the light fall on the just
and the unjust in a rain of impartial brightness.

For Frank O'Connor and Elizabeth Bowen, it is a part
of life itself. She sees it more softly than he does, more
like a transcendent mist, a haze that reveals the inward
nature of the transfigured thing or person. She shows a
particular sensitiveness to its softer, more subdued effects :
and if you read her account of a Dublin childhood,
" Seven Winters ", you will see why. She sees its
brilliant, triumphant passages—none better: but whereas
with O'Connor the light is sometimes cinematic, it
never is with her. And—this is the real point—for her,
it merges in the *characters*. It is part of the substance of
which they are made. They are not thrown into relief
by it. It shines through them, it enters into them at a
magical angle, it becomes part of their bloodstream ; it
is one of their faculties. In other words—and this is a
point I shall be returning to in a moment—all the elements
in a scene are considered : the focus is not exclusively on
the human participants. Or, should we say, the awareness that perceives what is happening is not limited by the
bodily boundaries of the characters, but flows beyond
them. Yet, all the time, it is intensely personal.

But let us be concrete, and look at examples of
Elizabeth Bowen's treatment of light. Here is one from
an early book, " The Last September ". The scene is
laid in Ireland.

" *Like splintered darkness, branches pierced the faltering
dusk of leaves. Evening drenched the trees ; the beeches were
soundless cataracts. Behind the trees, pressing in from the open
and empty country like an invasion, the orange bright sky crept
and smouldered. Firs, bearing up to pierce, melted against
the brightness Somewhere, there was a sunset in which the
mountains lay like glass.*

" *Dark had so gained the trees that Lois, turning back from
the window, was surprised at how light the room was. Day
still coming in from the fields by the south windows, was
stored in the mirrors, in the sheen of the wall-paper, so that
the room still shone* ".

In that passage you get not only an extreme sensitiveness
to light, and its concomitant shadow, but the appreciation
of its fluid quality, which is always present to the Irish
writer. Liquid light—luminous mist—and finally light
as an ingredient not only in human experience but in
the medium which experiences.

This awareness of light has been with Elizabeth Bowen
from the start. Take a few sentences at random from a
very early book, " Ann Lee's ", written over twenty
years ago. The first is about ladies' hats :—

" *These were the hats one dreamed about—no, even in a
dream one had never directly beheld them ; they glimmered
rather on the margin of one's dreams* ".

How essentially that shows her trademark : and how
close in it she is to James Joyce, the Joyce of " A Portrait
of the Artist as a Young Man ". Listen again to this,
also from " Ann Lee's ".—

" *Hewson's hand brushed across the switchboard, lights
would spring up dazzlingly against the ceiling and pour down
opulently on to the amber floor to play and melt among the
shadows of the feet* ".

That she wrote over twenty years ago. And this :—

" *When Mrs. Willand's parrot escaped, it rocketed in a
pale green streak across the sky and settled in the chestnut tree
at the foot of the garden, where it became invisible among the
branches* ".

Picture to yourself how the ordinary visual writer would have handled those experiences, and you will be on the way to realising what a special sensibility we are dealing with.

Now jump over a number of years, and come to one of the finest novels of our time, " The Death of the Heart ". So as not to press too hard on what I am after, let us take a passage describing light out of doors, a passage to match that first extract from " The Last September " :—

" *Thickets of hazel gauzed over the distances inside : boles of trees rose rounded out of the thickets into the spring air. Light, washing the stretching branches, sifted into the thickets, making a small green flame of every early leaf. Unfluting in the armpit warmth of the valley, leaves were still timid, humid : in the uphill woods spring still only touched the boughs in a green mist that ran into the sky* ".

This is more varied, more conscious ; the experience is on more than one plane. And, though in this passage only by an epithet, the identity between various forms of life is affirmed. The human sensitiveness has overrun its banks. The border line between one level of experience and another is disappearing into that green mist.

I could go on quoting examples of Elizabeth Bowen's preoccupation with light, but I will content myself with pointing out that the final catastrophe of Markie and Emmeline in " To the North " is told in terms of light that streams towards them as the road streams towards them, as distance and speed rush in a stream, as boundaries are crossed, as everything in an experience is related through a continuous fluid motion in space and time to what is on the other side of it.

Here are the final lines of a passage unequalled in its ecstacy of speed and light and the relationship of each moment to those that follow :—

" *He watched the next light dawn like doom, make a harsh aurora, bite into the road's horizon and, widening, flood the Great North Road from bank to bank. His fingers an inch from the wheel, wondering if he dared stun her, he said hopelessly : ' Emmeline . . .' with the last calm of impotence. As though hearing her name on his lips for the first time, dazzled, she turned to smile. Head-on, magnetised up the heart of the fan of approaching brightness, the little car, strung on speed, held unswerving way. Someone, shrieking, wrenched at a brake ahead : the great car, bounding, swerved on its impetus. Markie dragged their wheel left : like gnats the two hung in the glare with unmoving faces. Shocked by the moment, Emmeline saw what was past averting. She said : ' Sorry ', shutting her eyes* ".

Now let us consider a longer passage, again from that early book, " The Last September ". It is the opening of the section called " The Arrival of Mr. and Mrs. Montmorency ". I choose it because it shows in a clear and simple form the direction and genius of her method.

" *About six o'clock the sound of a motor, collected out of the wide country and narrowed under the trees of the avenue, brought the household out in excitement onto the steps. Up among the beeches, a thin iron gate twanged ; the car slid out from a net of shadow, down the slope to the house. Behind the flashing wind-screen Mr. and Mrs. Montmorency produced —arms waving and a wild escape to the wind of her mauve motor-veil—an agitation of greeting. They were long-promised visitors. They exclaimed, Sir Richard and Lady Naylor exclaimed and signalled : no one spoke yet. It was a moment of happiness, of perfection.*

" *In those days, girls wore crisp white skirts and transparent blouses clotted with white flowers ; ribbons, threaded through with a view to appearance, appeared over their shoulders. So that Lois stood at the top of the steps looking cool and fresh ; she knew how fresh she must look, like other young girls, and clasping her elbows tightly behind her back, tried hard to conceal her embarrassment. The dogs came pattering out from the hall and stood beside her ; above, the vast facade of the house stared coldly over its mounting lawns. She wished she could freeze the moment and keep it always. But as the car approached, as it stopped, she stooped down and patted one of the dogs.*

" *As the car drew up the Montmorencys unwound from their rugs. They stood shaking hands and laughing in the yellow theatrical sunshine. They had motored over from Carlow. Two toppling waves of excitement crashed and mingled ; for moments everyone was inaudible. Mrs. Montmorency looked up the steps. 'And this is the niece !' she exclaimed with delight. 'Aren't we dusty !' she added, as Lois said nothing. 'Aren't we too terribly dusty !' And a tired look came down at the back of her eyes at the thought of how dusty she was.*

" ' *She's left school now*', *said Sir Richard proudly.*

" ' *I don't think I should have known you*', *said Mr. Montmorency, who had not seen Lois since she was ten and evidently preferred children.*

" ' *Oh, I think she's the image of Laura—*'

" ' *But we have tea waiting. Are you really sure, now, you've had tea ?*'

" ' *Danielstown's looking lovely, lovely. One sees more from the upper avenue—didn't you clear some trees ?*'

" ' *The wind had three of the ashes—you came quite safe ? No trouble ? Nobody at the cross roads ? Nobody stopped you ?*'

" ' And are you sure about tea ? ' continued Lady Naylor. ' After all that—look, it's coming up now. No, Francie, don't be ridiculous ; come in now, both of you '.

" ' They swept in ; their exclamations, constricted suddenly, filled the hall. There was so much to say after twelve years : they all seemed powerless. Lois hesitated, went in after them and, as nobody noticed, came out again. The car with the luggage turned and went round to the back, deeply scoring the gravel. She yawned and looked out over the sweep to the lawn beyond, where little tufts of shadow pricked like reeds from water out of the flat gold light. Beyond the sunk fence, six Kerry cows followed each other across with wading steps and stood under a lime tree. All the way up the house the windows were open ; light came diagonally from window to window through corner rooms. Two storeys up, she could have heard a curtain rustle, but the mansion piled itself up in silence over the Montmorencys' voices.

" She yawned with reaction. It was simply the Montmorencys who had come ; whom all day one had been expecting. Yet she had been unable to read, had scattered unfinished letters over her table, done the flowers atrociously. Sweet-peas had spun and quivered between her fingers from their very importance . . . ' I apologise for the mauve sweet-peas ', she would have liked to be able to say to Mr. Montmorency. ' I don't care for mauve myself. I can't think why I ever picked them ; there were plenty of others. But, as a matter of fact, I was nervous '. And—' Nervous ? ' she would wish Mr. Montmorency to ask her searchingly, ' why ? ' But she had her reserves, even in imagination ; she would never tell him.

" But she had seen at once that Mr. Montmorency, who must be really so subtle, would not take the trouble to understand her ".

E

You will have heard in that the overtones and the undertones I have been talking about. They bring us, I think, to what Elizabeth Bowen is trying to do. If I am right, it is central and very important. She is trying to enlarge the range of human awareness. She is trying to treat each experience as a whole.

In the work of such an essentially English writer as Thomas Hardy, the characters in the midst of their emotional storm and stress look up and see their mood expressed in the torment of the skies. There is a correspondence between man's mood and nature. In Elizabeth Bowen's books this is more than a coincidence. The same impulse, the same fact is being expressed on two levels. We are shown a total experience. Life itself is manifest in sky and light and scene and characters all at once, and each manifestation is valid.

I am putting this clumsily. Let me try again. Suppose you are in a room with another person. A conversation takes place between you which is important for the whole of your life. Of that experience everything in the room is a part. The furniture, the unlit sticks in the grate, the motes dancing in the sunbeam that comes in at the window and falls on the pattern of the carpet, all belong to that experience. But ordinary human awareness is limited, specialised, blinkered. It concentrates on a fraction of the whole. Elizabeth Bowen's awareness is wider. She realises the experience as a whole, and tries to include as much of it as she can.

Everything she sees is seen through an intensely personal prism : thus far she is introverted. The external details are seen with a vivid and accurate eye : in that she is extraverted The human boundaries are overrun, the epithets are interchangeable—as when she talks of the " armpit warmth of the valley ".

Look at that strange short story, " Pink May ". A married woman, living with her husband in a furnished house, is in love with another man. Into her happiness intrudes the feeling that the furniture is watching her, and that the ghost of a woman who lived there before is wrecking the affair. Say, if you like, that her own unconscious mind is projecting on her surroundings the slow defeat of her happiness. The point is, that what happens comes from the situation as a whole, including the furniture, including the supposed ghost of the former occupant. Other stories show the same overflow. She is all the time trying to increase the range of human perception.

For her protagonist she selects the young girl: feminine sensitiveness uncorrupted by surrender to time. Lois in " The Last September ", Portia in " The Death of the Heart "—here is the human focus, the point of view, the perception by which the world is judged. Lois is right, rather than Mr. Montmorency. I have heard people call Portia's story and her flight to Major Brutt pathetic. That is the last thing it is. Tragic, if you like, but the tragedy is not Portia's. The tragedy is Major Brutt's and Anna's and St. Quentin's. Portia does not fail. It is they who fail. Hers is the untarnished viewpoint by which theirs is arraigned.

" Why could you not marry me ? " she asks Major Brutt. Why indeed ? Because he is caught in the net of time, and she not yet. Because living longer has not made him wiser, but limited his sensibility, narrowed the range of his response. There is a lot that Portia does not know, but she belongs to eternity. He and the others have surrendered to time.

It may seem a paradox that this supra-personal sensitiveness should at the same time be intensely personal. In

fact, there is no paradox. Just as the personal vision of
anyone deeply in love is not diminished but enlarged by
learning to give sovereign value to another personality,
so the personal vision of these characters of Elizabeth
Bowen's, or rather the personal vision we are made to
share when we read her—is enlarged and strengthened
by its commerce with the other elements in a situation.
" It is the haunted who haunt ", she says in a recent
short story. Exactly. There is always a two-way traffic
between her and the world around her. Perception
circulates between the two. And she is using every
means to intensify the traffic. Look at her invocation of
the ghost in her latest book of short stories, " The Demon
Lover ". The ghost in " Pink May " may, as I suggested,
be a projection of the woman's unconscious mind, or an
emanation from the furniture, or the actual ghost of a
previous tenant. You can take your pick : but under
any label it remains a fresh medium of perception. The
ghost in " Green Holly " goes further : but for our
purposes it is enough to say that, in this story, perception
spreads like a pool both in time and space, overrunning
the boundaries of Messrs. Rankstock and Winterslow
and the egregious Miss Bates.

Do not let me seem to suggest that Elizabeth Bowen
is in any sense a nebulous writer. She is extremely, often
devilishly precise. She can most fearsomely describe a
cad—a power shared by E. M. Delafield. She knows
how men talk when they are by themselves, as does a
writer who does not otherwise resemble her, Norah
Hoult. She hates practical, successful, extraverted people
with a cold ferocity that puts her on the introvert side
of the fence. She has a most subtle ear for those
inflections of speech which show reserves and ambiguities
beneath.

She can suggest disquiet, whether moral, physical, or psychic, to a degree unequalled among her contemporaries. She can convey the very texture and perfume of happiness. All these things are the result of a merciless and unfaltering precision of awareness and of expression. All belong to what, for me at least, is the essential quality of her work; illumination. In the work of no other modern writer is so clear, so various a light thrown upon experience. Marvell's phrase " The Various Light " might have been made to describe her writing. She is an artist of very rare quality. Her achievement is memorable, and all lovers of fine writing await her future in a confident excitement.

WYNDHAM LEWIS

by GEOFFREY GRIGSON

WYNDHAM LEWIS—it is a bigger statement than it sounds—is a writer who is not for sale. Most things and most writers, wriggle as they may, are for sale ; the purchasers are you, me, the state, business journalism, the B.B.C., anything which, at any time, nourishes the lowest common multiple of demand.

The State says " write me a propoganda article " and the writer agrees ; business says " paint me an advertisement ", the artist agrees—until even the talented writer or the talented artist is, in a varying part of his existence, a Public Relations Officer ; a salesman who sells part of himself for an end which has nothing to do with himself, nothing to do with the values he believes to be valuable.

One does not become a bought writer, or a bought artist, only by writing or painting something *ad hoc*. One can write or paint as the majority write or paint. One can sell the substance of one's being as an artist or a writer to the lowest common multiple of intellectual level and sentiment and compromise and dishonesty. One can fail, as most of us do, to resist the immensely heavy pressures of our time which force one down to that l.c.m.

Wyndham Lewis has resisted those pressures. Many years ago he wrote a pamphlet, " The Code of the Herdsman " : the Herdsman lived on the mountain, the herd lived on the plain. The mountain was not an Ivory Tower insulated from the herd. Since the mountain rose up out of the plain, and the herdsman was born out of the herd, since herd and herdsman both belonged to humanity, it was necessary for the herdsman to include in his strict code of behaviour an amount of contact with the herd, with the plains people. I mention that to show that there is nothing solipsist or anti-human, or isolationist, about Wyndham Lewis's writings : they are not soft, tender, flattering : they are tough, but they are concerned with humanity ; though the writer sticks to his code ; and the code says " do not sell yourself : do not be a bought man ".

Let me illustrate one kind of bought man, one kind of transaction, from the past—the transaction of selling the *way* one writes or paints. I mean the case of Sir John Everett Millais. As a young man he had painted truly. In 1886 he painted a picture of his grandson blowing bubbles. He sold the picture to a journalist for reproduction in his popular journal. The journalist used "Bubbles" in that way ; and then sold the picture again to a firm of soap-makers, and the soap-makers made "Bubbles" into an advertisement. Millais was angry and protested. He had not—so he must have thought— sold himself to advertising soap. But he had : he had sold himself to soap, by selling the substance of his being as an artist to the l.c.m. of demand, by painting just such a picture, in just such a manner, as was suitable for advertising soap. By the way, Millais's biographer made just that defence by which so many people, now, justify the almost universal habit of the artist selling himself to

advertising—that the example set by the soap makers
" has tended to raise the character of our illustrated
advertisements, whether in papers or posters ".

This is the point for introducing a piece from Wyndham
Lewis himself—a piece from " Time and Western Man "
on the principle of advertisement, the principle of
salesmanship in modern life :

" *The traditional Yankee method of Advertisement suggests
a credulity, a love of sensation and an absence of background in
the submissive, hypnotised public, that could justly claim to be*
unexampled, *and as beating anything ever heard of before in
recorded history. But that method is now in universal use.*

" *It promises* monts et merveilles *every instant of the day.
It has battered and deadened every superlative so much that
superlatives no longer in themselves convey anything. All
idea of a true value—of any scale except the pragmatic scale of
hypnotism and hoax—is banished for ever from the life of the
great majority of people living in the heart of an advertising
zone, such as any great modern city. They are now almost
entirely incapable of anything except sensation ; for to think is
to be able to traverse the scale of values from the nadir to the
zenith. The world of superlatives is a monotonous horizontal
drumming on the top note, from which an insistent, intoxicating
time can be extracted, but nothing else. So Advertisement
fulfils all the requirements of the general definition of
'* romance *' ".*

Now Wyndham Lewis, susceptible as he is to wonder,
capable as he is of attraction by the exotic culture of the
Incas of Peru, or by the solid enigmas of the statues of
Easter Island, equally capable as he is of summarising
G. K. Chesterton as " a fierce, foaming Toby jug ", and
of summarising Keats in a phrase from his one long poem,
asking " what page the sorcerer John Keats tore from the

shut book "—Wyndham Lewis, in spite of all these tastes, is not on the side of sensation, intoxication, or romance. He pairs with the solid, and not with the liquid, the outside, and not the inside, with reason and not the disorderly mess of first impressions. Lewis says this, in " Men Without Art " :

" *The pretentions of art, I take it, do not point to anything beyond the thresholds of life, or aspire to transcend the well-defined limits of man's animal status. An animal in every respect upon the same footing as a rat or an elephant, I imagine you will agree—man, except for what the behaviourist terms his word-habit—is that and no more, except for his paradoxical 'reason'. So really the word—in contrast to the sound or image—is the thing most proper and peculiar to him*".

The *word*, the rational statement, in contrast to the sound or image. So in the arts, generally and in his own practice of the arts, Wyndham Lewis is against salesmanship, is against, as he says, " ecstatic propaganda . . . . plunges into cosmic streams of flux or time ".

" I have ", he declares, " other views on the subject of attaining perfection. I prefer the chaste wisdom of the Chinese or the Greek, to that hot, tawny brand of superlative fanaticism coming from the parched deserts of the Ancient East, with its ineradicable abstractness. I am for the physical world ".

As the Enemy, Lewis is for the eye, for the " things of vision " : as the Enemy, he is against a great many things ; against the proletarianised art dealing with the will-less men *to whom things are done ;* against the intestinal stream-of-feeling art, of Joyce, or Virginia Woolf, or D. H. Lawrence ; against the child-art, the art of what he called the " eternal sucklings "—he has included among them Picasso as well as Charlie Chaplin.

He is against the romantic, the automatic, the solipsist, the sensational, the aesthetic, the thrill, the disordered, whether from the Marquis de Sade or, I suppose, from the neo-romantic, the apocalyptic, the gut poets so much in vogue at this moment.

In short, he is for service to that reason by which, as he says, animal man recognises his animal status. And I can imagine his contempt—justified, rational contempt, by which man orders his inescapable animality—for some of the poetry which it seems we must hear broadcast and discussed with solemnity in this Third Programme ; as well as his contempt for that clinching, astonishing statement on modern poetry which we have lately had (so far do such attitudes go) from the Oxford Professor of Poetry—the statement, the approving statement, that " the modern conception of poetry is of something . . . which gives an immediate, overwhelming thrill "—that for modern poets " the thrill is what matters, and they think it foolish to talk about techniques or taste except with reference to this end ".

To go back to my first quotation from Lewis : " All idea of a true value—of any scale except the pragmatic scale of hypnotism and hoax—is banished for ever from the life of the great majority of people living in the heart of an advertising zone "—living, one can add, in the heart of a zone which advertises the supreme, poetical merit of thrill and sensation. For Lewis the one general law in art is " to sharpen your taste and intelligence "— taste *and* intelligence—" in every way that you can ".

Being for the eye, for the physical world, as against the dark juices and the flux, means that in everything— in his novels, his criticism, his poetry, Wyndham Lewis uses the physical, uses the things which are seen, to convey even the things which cannot be seen, thoughts, emotions, argument.

The description of G. K. Chesterton as a "fierce, foaming toby-jug" is a simple example of his method, of its lucidity, its vigour and economy. After dealing with the "ninetyish", the feminine, aestheticism of the flux, in "Men Without Art", Lewis wrote : "It has been with considerable shaking in my shoes, and a feeling of treading upon a carpet of eggs, that I have taken the cow by the horns in this chapter".

In "Tarr", the German artist fixes, in that enormously comic scene of the dance at the Bonnington Club, on "a flapper radiant with heavy inexperience and loaded with bristling bronze curls"; and this is how he describes Frederick Tarr himself walking with his Russian girl :,

"*He swam with ease beside his big hysterical black swan, seeming to guide her with a golden halter. They were swimming with august undulations of thought across the Luxembourg Gardens on this sunny and tasteful evening about four o'clock*".

In fact, a longer passage from "Tarr" will explain much about Lewis's writing and attitude. It will explain his word habit, his habit of fashioning meaning and action out of the material of language. Tarr is pitching in to Alan Hobson; well-to-do, idle, long-haired, shabbily dressed, a type of our time like the Public Relations Officer, one of the pretence artists who have invaded art like viruses. Tarr has just condemned Hobson as—it is an unforgettable phrase—" a scare-crow of an advanced fool-farm ".

"'*Wait a minute*' Hobson said, with a laugh. '*You accuse me of sentimentality in my choice of costume. I wonder if you are as free from sentimentality*'.

"'*I don't care a tinker's blue curse about that—I am talking about you—let me proceed—with your training—you are decked in the plumes of very fine birds indeed. But your plumes are not meant to fly with, but merely to slouch and skip along the surface of the earth. You wear the livery of a ridiculous set, you are a cunning and sleek domestic. No thought can come out of your head before it has slipped on its uniform. All your instincts are drugged with a malicious langour, a charm, a respectability, invented by a set of old women and mean, cadaverous little boys'.*

" Hobson opened his mouth, had a movement of the body to speak. But he relapsed.

" ' You reply, ' what is all this fuss about ? I have done the best for myself—I was not suited for any heroic station, like yours. I live sensibly and quietly, cultivating my vegetable ideas, and also my roses and Victorian lilies—I do no harm to anybody'.

" ' That is not quite the case. That is a little inexact. Your proceedings possess a herdesque astuteness ; in the scale against the individual weighing less than the Yellow Press, yet being a closer and meaner attack. Also you are essentially spies, in a scurvy, safe and well-paid service, as I told you before. You are disguised to look like the thing it is your function to betray— what is your position ?—you have bought for eight hundred pounds at an aristocratic educational establishment a complete mental outfit, a programme of manners. For four years you trained with other recruits. You are now a perfectly disciplined social unit, with a profound esprit de corps. The Cambridge set that you represent is, as observed in an average specimen, a cross between a Quaker, a Pederast, and a Chelsea artist. Your Oxford brothers, dating from the Wilde decade, are a stronger body. The Chelsea artists are much less flimsy. The Quakers are powerful rascals. You represent, my Hobson, the dregs of Anglo-Saxon civilisation !—There is nothing softer on earth—your flabby portion is a mixture of the lees of Liberalism, the poor froth blown off the decadent nineties,*

*the wardrobe-leavings of a vulgar Bohemianism with its
headquarters in Chelsea!*

" ' *You are concentrated, systematic slop—there is nothing
in the universe to be said for you. Any efficient state would
confiscate your property, burn your wardrobe, that old hat,
and the rest, as* infecte *and insanitary, and prohibit you from
propagating*'.

" *Tarr's white collar shone dazzlingly in the sun—his
bowler hat bobbed and cut clean lines as he spoke.*

" ' *A breed of mild pervasive cabbages has set up a wide and
creeping rot in the West of Europe. They make it indirectly
a peril and tribulation for living things to remain in the
neighbourhood. You are systematizing and vulgarising the
individual. You are not an individual. You have, I repeat
no right to that hair and that hat. You are trying to have the
apple and eat it too. You should be in uniform, and at work,
not* uniformly *out of uniform, and libelling the Artist by
your idleness. Are you idle?* '

" *Tarr had drawn up short, turned squarely on Hobson;
in an abrupt and disconnected voice he asked his question . .*"

That strikes me as energetic, entertaining, cleansing
satire—a description you can extend to all Lewis's best
writing. And the point is this : all Lewis's best writing—
article, pamphlet, story, treatise, all his work is, in fact,
one work, built up on a developing system of ideas and
of vital expressions for those ideas. I should call that
work a vast, Herculean cleansing work, aimed at showing
art as, in Wyndham Lewis's description, " a constant
stronghold of the purest human consciousness ". For
the last thirty years Lewis has fought to exhibit that
stronghold, and incidentally to cleanse it, by sharp-edged
satirical laughter, of all the tumble-down suburbs, the
tin shacks, the allotments, the iron bed-steads, built up

and laid out all around it, the suburbs inhabited by all
the varieties of the salesman and the art parasite, the Alan
Hobsons and the pretence artists (all, as he says, " Wine,
Womanry and Free-verse-cum-soda-water "), all the
pseudo-artists of collective hypnotism, all the artists who
exclusively cultivate the " wild body ". The wild body
—of course there's plenty of the " wild body " in Lewis
himself—is the rich, inescapable fact about the human
animal, it. is man's animal status. " But the work of
art ", as Lewis has said, " does the reordering "—the
reordering of the sensations—" in the interest of the
intellect as well as of the emotions ".

If we could have a collected edition of Wyndham
Lewis—a collecting of novels, stories, criticism, treatises,
essays which never have been collected—we should
understand, as perhaps some of us don't want to understand,—his immense unity ; his immense importance in
a time of flux and foolishness. I would say meanwhile
that you can find much of the necessary Lewis in two
books alone—in " Tarr "—an early novel, but it is one
of the most rounded, energetic, commanding things he
has achieved ; and in his treatise of " Time and
Western Man ".

I. COMPTON-BURNETT

by EDWARD SACKVILLE-WEST

WHAT DO YOU EXPECT of a contemporary novel?
A reflection of your own life, with the events and feelings
keyed up a little higher—made rather more exciting than
you have ever found them? Or a picture of life as you
would like it to be? Or merely an escape into an ideal
world which never could be? I ask these questions, not
because I can answer them, but because it depends on
your answer whether or not you will enjoy the novels of
the very peculiar—in fact, the *unique*—writer whose
quality I want to describe.

Miss Ivy Compton-Burnett is the author of some ten
novels, superficially very similar, with titles like
"Brothers and Sisters", "Parents and Children",
"Elders and Betters", "Daughters and Sons".

The scene in which these stories are always set is a
smallish English country house, with its village, its church
and parson, and a few near neighbours, all living the
sequestered life of the English countryside between, say
1880 and 1914. The world—you may guess—of Jane
Austen, of George Eliot, of Mrs. Gaskell. But with this
difference,—that the plots which involve that outwardly
quiet and orderly world are violent and dramatic in the
extreme.

The grizzliest of skeletons lurk in the cupboards of these large, comfortable, and highly articulate families. Their rattling usually begins to be heard when someone or other arrives from the outside world and disturbs the delicate order of the household. Then there is, literally, the devil to pay. Murder, suicide, immolation, mental cruelty, burning of important letters, suppression of legal papers—there are few crimes which these people do not commit, and none at all (we feel) of which they would not be capable, on occasion. For these stories are psychological thrillers conducted on the highest plane of intellectual brilliance. As in the novels of Henry James, Miss Compton-Burnett's characters all speak in the same way, and all are artists in words. We distinguish them by what they do and say, and by what is said about them by other characters, but not by their manner of speech. This procedure is, of course, a convention, and one which many people may find hard to accept—especially if they are accustomed to the shorthand dialogue of the average realistic novel. But anybody who is used to enjoying the verbal wit and eloquence of Elizabethan drama will have no difficulty in accepting Miss Compton-Burnett's literary convention.

In a moment I will give you some examples of that verbal wit which is the most constant feature of these novels ; but first I want to make one or two further points. To begin with, each book consists, almost exclusively, of *dialogue*.

What description there may be is reduced to the absolute minimum needed to tell us who is speaking and where they are situated. The physical appearance of the characters is given, once for all, at their first entrance into the story. The setting of the novel—the look of the the house, its date, its surroundings and so on—is plainly

and straightforwardly stated, in the fewest possible words.
There is no impressionistic writing in any of this ; it is
all as bare as the stage directions in a play. And indeed
these novels do constantly remind us of plays. Miss
Compton-Burnett's method is purely dramatic in effect,
although her dialogue does not have—and is not inetnded
to have—the concision of stage conversation.

But now for some examples. The first is from the
beginning of " Daughters and Sons ". In all novels
which deal with leisured people, the scenes tend to
gravitate round the meal table, and many of Miss
Compton-Burnett's most dramatic—as well as funniest
—conversations, take place at breakfast. The tyrant of
the household (there always is one—in this case a
grandmother) is usually the first down, waiting to tick
off the children (grown up or not) for lateness. Here
is Mrs. Ponsonby dealing with her grandson, and her
grand-daughter, Clare.*

MRS. PONSONBY : *Chilton, what is your age ?*

CHILTON : *Eighteen and two months, Grandma. There are
sixty-four years between us. It makes us such good compan-
ions.*

MRS. PONSONBY : *Then must you carve a cold pheasant as if
you were ten years less ? Do you suppose no one wants any
breast but yourself ?*

CHILTON : *I hope no one does. Victor knows he has no claim
to any.*

MRS. PONSONBY : *Did it not occur to you to offer it first to
your sisters ?*

CHILTON : *I believe you see what occurred to me. There was
not much of it.*

MRS. PONSONBY : *And so you took it for yourself ?*

---

* *For the reader's convenience we have set out these extracts in acting form—Editor.*

F

CHILTON : *So I did. You tell me I must earn my bread, and that made me think of having some pheasant with it.*

MRS. PONSONBY : *Did you suppose the others were tired of pheasant ?*

CHILTON : *I suppose they were tired of these. In fact, I knew they were.*

MRS. PONSONBY : *You may think you are funny, Chilton. I can assure you no one agrees with you.*

CHILTON : *Muriel does. I hear the sound of her young laughter.*

MRS. PONSONBY : *She has the tricks of her age. Giggling happens to be one of them. It is a nervous habit which we must hope she will leave behind.*

CLARE : *It is hard to see how we can leave behind nervous habits. Probably most of our habits are of that nature.*

From that fragment of talk you can get the astringent taste of Miss Compton-Burnett's style. All her chief characteristics are there : the surface is urbane, the emotional control perfect. The speaker may be irritated but does not fail to keep a sharp ear open for the exact meaning of what is said. The younger members of the family are determined to keep their own end up while paying verbal respect to their elders. A few scattered pieces of repartee will complete these points. Here is one, from " Men and Wives " :

" ' *I don't dare to think what your father would have said* '.
" ' *I don't know why, as he can't say it* ' ".

Or take this, from " Elders and Betters ", in which a father is twitting his son with neglecting his duties as tutor to a small boy :

" ' *What would Anna say to your methods ?* '
" ' *She would think that Uncle Benjamin ought not to pay me* '.

" ' *And do you think he ought ?* '

" ' *Well, my service is of a kind that cannot be paid for in money, and that means that it is paid for in that way, but not very well* ' ".

Or this, from " Parents and Children " :

" ' *Why does one dislike the term, bride, as applied to one's mother ?* '

" ' *There are several reasons, and none of them can be mentioned* ' ".

I think you will agree with me that this kind of thing is extremely funny ; but don't run away with the idea that Miss Compton-Burnett is a heartless or superficial writer, cracking smart epigrams while her characters suffer torture. It is true that she is consistently and wonderfully clever, but never *merely* so : the tennis-rally wit which she puts into the mouths of her people operates with equally devastating effect at all levels of feeling, from the affectionate banter of the brothers and sisters who throng these books, to the eloquent speech of experienced adults who find themselves caught in the toils of their own egotism and ruthlessness. For in these stories each person depends upon the others for the exact quality of his or her own expression. As in a piece of musical counterpoint, the harmony or disharmony is determined by the position of *all* the parts at any given moment. So that Miss Compton-Burnett's characters are only secondarily individuals : primarily they are sons, daughters, wives, fathers, illegitimate cousins, and so forth. The family occupies the position assumed, in other novels, by society in general. The earlier and more tragic books tighten the noose round the family, isolating it ; while the later novels—" Parents and Children ", " Elders and Betters "—which are much lighter in tone, loosen the tie and allow the characters to flow out, at least by implication, into the outside world. A passage from "Daughters and Sons" makes this point with overtones of precise bitterness. The Vicar, Dr. Chaucer, is speaking to Miss Hallam, the new governess in the Ponsonby household :—

" ' You do not tell me you would rather be a stranger in the house than a member of it' ?

" ' I would much rather ; I could not bear to be a member. You do not know what it is like'.

" ' You may say it, but the heart knoweth its own bitterness. What is a little impatience, hastiness—tyranny, if it must be said, compared with a real isolation and loneliness ? "

" ' I am afraid it must be said, and they are a great deal worse ' ".

Yet no one in these books willingly abandons his family, and the tyranny of its head, in order to live alone. It seems as if, for these subtle and searching people, the family were the one and only source of value—of life. That is why they are all so careful to preserve its fabric intact, at almost any cost. Whatever happens—however much or long they may suffer—they must not say the really disruptive thing, the thing to which there is no verbal answer. No one ever says to the family tyrant— to the matriarchal Mrs. Ponsonby, to Sophia Stace in " Brothers and Sisters ", to Duncan Edgeworth in " A House and its Head "—no one ever says in so many words to these monstrous egotists : " You make our lives intolerable ".

We long for their victims to say this—perhaps think it unnatural they never lose their tempers, at any rate with the person who matters most. Then we realise that this insistence on good manners is the high tension wire along which all civilised social life proceeds, and to which it must keep on pain of electrocution. Family life, if it is to hold together at all, does not permit loss of control on any issue except a side issue. The centre must on no account be allowed to fall apart ; and the centre is always somebody who exacts a greater tribute than is due to him—in fact, more or less of a tyrant. The most perfect example of this high tension is the dreadful Duncan Edgeworth—the Victorian father at his most unreasonable, inconsiderate and despotic.

" A House and Its Head " is one of Miss Compton-Burnett's largest books and the lower reaches of it take us into the extremes of horror and tragedy. But, although Mr. Edgeworth is never less than utterly detestable, we are constantly being amused by the absurd flights of his irresponsible egotism. Take, for instance, the priceless scene where he indulges to the full his childish passion for teasing his family—keeping them on tenterhooks, nagging and nudging them, daring them to lose their tempers and so to justify him in being even more disagreeable than usual. Preparing to leave the the house on a visit to his sister, Mr. Edgeworth leads his nephew, Grant, and his daughter, Sybil, a final dance before getting into the carriage which is waiting to take him to the station. I have abridged the passage a little, for convenience in reading.

MR. EDGEWORTH : *Grant ! Fetch my writing case from my desk ; and put in some pens and stamps, and bring it up here ! I have been calling until I am hoarse ; I thought you were all stone deaf.*

GRANT : *It was odd to continue calling.*

MR. EDGEWORTH : *Grant ! Grant ! Don't you hear me ? Can't you answer me, boy ?*

GRANT : *I am getting the things, Uncle ! I will be up in a minute.*

MR. EDGEWORTH : *But can't you answer me ? Can't you open your mouth to reply, when I stand and shout myself hoarse ? Are you dumb as well as deaf ?*

GRANT : *I thought you would know I was getting the case, Uncle.*

MR. EDGEWORTH : *How was I to know, when I shouted and got no response ? How was I to guess at what moment I should pierce your senses ? How was I to know you had any senses, when there was no evidence of it ?*

(*Grant ran upstairs and offered the case, Sibyl on his heels with its supplies. Something in the zeal attending these offices caused Duncan to meet them with deliberation*).

MR. EDGEWORTH : *Pens ; stamps ; yes. Paper ? Do I want paper ? Will not your aunt have that, Sibyl ? That is—ha ! ha !—if I get there, and need it.*

SIBYL : *Of course she will, Father. How stupid of me ! I will take it back and look round to see if there is anything else.*

MR. EDGEWORTH : *There is no reason for hurry : I don't want the final look round made yet. We may never get to it. Who knows ?* (*Yawns, sighs*). *So many things come in the way of really getting off, more than the business is worth.*

(*He broke off and looked up and down a newspaper from a trunk, smiling to himself at its reminders*).

MR. EDGEWORTH : *Has anyone seen my old gloves, that I wear in the grounds ? Those that are kept in the drawer in the hall, or should be kept there. I know people are always disturbing that drawer.*

SIBYL : *They are not there, Father !*

MR. EDGEWORTH : *Of course they are not there ! If they were there, should I ask you if you had seen them ? I should simply tell you to fetch them.*

(*This was accepted as true*).

SIBYL : *I thought you wanted them fetched, Father.*
MR. EDGEWORTH : *Of course I wanted them fetched. If I did not, should I have asked about them ? I should not expect them to walk to me, should I ? Or to fly to my hand ?*
SIBYL : *Why you have them in your hand, Father, waving them about.**

It is part of Miss Compton-Burnett's strength that she is never afraid that by displaying her tragic figures in a farcical light she may diminish their stature for us. If she were a less consistent stylist, this might happen ; but I think it never does. If you can accept the convention at all you will be able to take the swift transitions from comedy to tragedy and back, without any feeling of strain or incredulity. In fact, " transition " is not really the right term to use in this connection. In all these novels it is taken for granted that the spoken word is adequate to deal with any situation, however appalling. " People do not feel as much as you want them to ", says one of her characters. This statement is like the arrow on a thermometer which marks 98.4 degrees.

It is because Miss Compton-Burnett assumes the truth of that statement that her plots are designed to bring the maximum of strain to bear upon the emotions of the people involved in them. In " Men and Wives " a mother, corroded by self-pity, attempts, and fails, to commit suicide, in order to attract all her family's attention to herself. So her eldest son poisons her, to put an end to her misery and his. In " More Women than Men " the jealous headmistress of a school murders a girl by exposing her, while suffering from pneumonia, to a draught of icy air. In " Daughters and Sons " the eldest daughter pretends to have committed suicide in order to shock her family into according her the position

---

* *Here again we have transferred the passage into acting form—Editor.*

of authority she covets and has lost. In " Brothers and
Sisters " a woman, Sophia Stace, conceals what she
imagines to be her father's will and is led by this act into
marrying her half-brother, who is known as her father's
adopted son and bears his name. Years later, the husband,
Christian Stace, discovers the letter revealing the truth
of his position, and dies of shock. You may think this
unlikely concatenation quite enough in itself for the plot
of a novel ; but Miss Compton-Burnett has added yet
a further complication. In the course of the book a
widow with grown-up children comes to live in the
village, and two of these children get engaged to marry
two of the young Staces—only to find their mother is
also Christian Stace's mother, so that in fact they are
proposing to marry their own nephew and neice. Im-
probable ? Absurd ? Well, perhaps. Truth is always
said to be stranger than fiction. But all this means is
that some real events make unsuitable material for works
of art. To me, I confess, it has often seemed that fiction
—the best fiction—is stranger than truth, but not for
that reason incompatible with it.

After all, plausibility of *plot* has always been thought
quite unimportant by the greatest novelists—by Balzac,
for instance, and Dickens, Hardy, Henry James. Truth
to the basic patterns of life, and to the quality of human
feeling—that is what the imaginative writer is always
after ; and these ends are best served by plots which are
metaphorical—or symbolic, if you prefer it—rather than
by those which stick closer to ordinary experience. Plots
which are devised as pretexts for religious or political
moralising fit the characters who illustrate them about as
well as a coat-hanger fits a coat ; but no better. For
Miss Compton-Burnett the plot has a much ampler
function: it is the apparatus which steadies the emotional

momentum—like the gyroscope in a flying bomb, or the hard pellet in the centre of a golf ball. And round that centre she winds the elastic of her wit and her human perception, so that the novel—like the golf ball—may fly smooth and straight to its goal. I have said that Miss Compton-Burnett is not a heartless writer, but in case any of you are still doubting that statement, I want to corroborate it by a passage from the end of " Brothers and Sisters ".

The terrible truth is out at last—the truth of which Sophia Stace, as well as her husband, will die, and her children, Andrew, Dinah, and Robin, are facing all that and more, since to them their mother is in herself a problem :

" *The next morning at breakfast Sophia looked ill and old. She hardly tried to eat, and her hands trembled over her tasks at the head of the table. Dinah offered to deal with them for her.*

" ' *No, no, darling, I can look after you all just a little while longer. I will care for you while I can* '.

" *She smiled, but in a minute gave it up, and sought her children's faces.*

" ' *I don't know how to describe my state to you. I know you must be worn out by my griefs and troubles ; but I must depend on your love. It is the only basis of my tottering life, the one thing that holds me from falling into the abyss. A great oppression still seems to be over me, a great cloud. It is as if I could not get strength to rise out of it, struggle as I will. And I have not striven so very hard. It may be that my struggling time is past. It is not only that I feel as if my days on earth were numbered, though I think they must be numbered now* '.

" *She smiled, and her children saw that she did not believe what she said, though they were beginning to believe it.*

" ' It is that I feel that this great blackness has come between Father and myself ; as if this that we were to each other, has taken away all our romance from us. As if, when I go to join him, there will stand a barrier between us. Though, if I had let the truth be discovered, we could not have had each other, not as we did. I could not have been your mother, you dear children of our love. I don't know where to turn my eyes for light. My way is dark, as I go alone into the valley of the shadow '.

" ' Your oratory is most telling ', said Andrew.

" Sophia laughed, and her eyes had a flash for a moment.

" ' In some countries it has been normal for children of the same father to marry ', said Dinah. ' There is no need to take too much of its happening once '.

" ' Dear one, what helpful things you do think of ! Doesn't she, Andrew ? Well, I must give myself up to trying to get better for all your sakes. I must resolve to think of nothing but that '.

" She glanced at Robin.

" ' Don't you want me to get well, then, Robin ? '

" Robin's fleeting thought had crossed his face. It was one of many, at variance with themselves.

" ' What a question to ask ! ' he said. ' I shall not answer it '.

" He was silent to the end of the meal.

" ' Really, Sophia cannot wonder if we rejoice sometimes at the prospect of freedom ', he said, when they were upstairs.

" ' She doesn't wonder, evidently ', said Dinah. ' She took to the idea readily when it was presented to her '.

" ' You might draw a veil over your moment of inner gladness ' said Andrew.

" ' I own the thought did cross my mind ', said Robin, ' As I say, how can it not at times '.

" ' *See it doesn't disfigure your face again* ' *said Dinah.*

" ' *Sophia believed my implied lie* ', *said Robin ;* ' *and it was only partly a lie* '.

" ' *Sophia is always soothed by lies* ', *said Andrew,* ' *even by whole ones, as I suspect she took yours to be* '.

" *Patty came in, and stood before them, shutting the door behind her.*

" ' *What have you been talking about at breakfast ? The maid who was doing the hall came down to the kitchen with a regular muddle of a tale. It will be out all over the place if you are not careful. It is all but out now. I did my best to put them all off, but I don't know how far I have done it* '.

" ' *Oh, well, Patty, if people will listen at doors, we are helpless* ', *said Dinah.* ' *We can't allow for that, though it does seem the rule of the house. And we have to talk to Sophia about it. She can't keep it off her mind. How is she to make an effort now, for the first time in her life ? If people will leave no stone unturned, to find out what they ought not to know, they must go on turning stones. There are some more to turn. Sophia must be served until the end* ' ".

In that passage, I think you will agree, the mask of humour is dropped, because the characters are no longer completely in control of the situation. They are still capable of irony, but they are feeling too deeply—and their creator with them—to try to retrieve their balance by flippancy. The verbal adroitness and precision is as astonishing as ever, but it is hoisted into eloquence— especially in Sophia's case—by a consciousness of dignity. " People do not feel as much as you want them to ". If this be true, it is a matter for rejoicing ; but at least the people in these stories never try to feel less than they can bear ; and that is as much as we have a right to expect.

Now, if you asked me to describe the quality of Miss Compton-Burnett's art by comparison with writers of the past, I should refer you to Meredith rather than to Henry James, and beyond him to the classical French dramatists, Racine and Molière. She inherits their pre-occupation with the temperature of the words and phrases we use in speech, and consequently with the temperature of the feelings they express.

Her books have the uniformity we are accustomed to associate with the more formal arts—abstract painting, sculpture, metaphysical poetry ; and her faults—for like other good writers Miss Compton-Burnett has faults— are all by-products of the single aim to which her art confines itself. Her plots are not easy to remember in detail ; the subsidiary characters are often too many in number and too dim in outline ; and particularly in her earlier novels I think she fills her canvas too rapidly, so that the reader becomes confused among so many people all talking alike. Her dialogue has, so to speak, only one gear—and that a very high one—this makes her books somewhat tiring to read, because it demands from the reader a constant degree of attention.

Of course it is open to anyone to reject work which displays these faults ; but to do so in this case is to deprive oneself of a pleasure as extraordinary, in its way, and as acute, as the pleasure to be derived from any highly stylised art. Like the seventeenth century dramatists with whom I have compared her, Miss Compton-Burnett makes do with a stage that is set once for all, and so does not distract her—or us—from exploring the intricacies of the private life. She is not in any obvious sense a topical writer ; but only the most bigoted person would blame her for that. To address yourself narrowly to the present is almost certainly to court a speedy oblivion.   Those who care little for quick returns, but strive in their art to catch only the unchanging essence of life, establish a lien on posterity ; and it is this type of artist to which Ivy Compton-Burnett unquestionably and unflinchingly belongs.

E. M. FORSTER

by ROSE MACAULAY

IF YOU ASKED a selection of educated English readers of fiction to pick out our most distinguished living novelist, nine out of ten, I should say, would answer E. M. Forster.

Literary reputations are seldom particularly just, so much depends on herd fashion and sadly inadequate individual perceptiveness. But E. M. Forster's reputation in this country—growing, perhaps, even now, though his last novel was published, alas, twenty-two years ago, and his first over forty—is nicely adjusted to his deserts.

As to his influence, very few sensitive writers of his own or of later generations can have escaped it altogether ; only those whose minds were tuned on to quite other wave-lengths. One has even heard him called " the father of the twentieth century novel ". It sounds a little portentous, but one sees the point ; though I would rather describe him as a piper playing a new kind of tune, which set those who liked it dancing in a new rhythm. It was a tune subtle and charming—much too charming, some austere critics have held. A recent writer on Mr. Forster says " On the question of Forster's famous charm, I find myself endorsing Laura Riding's remarks concerning " A Room with a View ".

" Before reading this book " (says Miss Riding) " I had met Mr. Forster and found him charming ; the book was recommended to me by my friends as a charming book. I read it. I could not deny that it was charming. Yet to me it was unpleasantly painful to read. It was too charming ".

The writer who thus quotes Miss Riding has some odd comments of his own on Mr. Forster, whom he regards as writing so much within the circumscribed limits of a bourgeois capitalist society, and being so much concerned with the lives of the irresponsible, moneyed, parasitical bourgeoisie, that all the spiritual conflicts and personal relationships that he portrays must be " false ", because "based on social falsehood". "False" is here, apparently used in a peculiar sense, and seems to mean " reprehensible ", or perhaps unimportant. Anyhow the writer's idea is that any spiritual struggle on the part of members of the middle classes which does not result in the repudiation of the false social order is invalidated, and any valid moral system among the bourgeoisie impossible.

Criticism on this level needn't be taken very seriously ; it is the kind of standard which is being now applied in Russia to artists. Applied to E. M. Forster, it is more than usually absurd, since he is the champion of individuals, of personal relationships, of private life. More than any other, I suppose, that is his theme.

" It is private life that holds out the mirror to infinity ; personal intercourse, and that alone, that ever hints at personality beyond our daily vision ".

No wonder that those who pin their faith to the social struggle and the class war, are annoyed by a writer who wrote some years ago, in 1939, when every one's mind was fixed on the horrors, the hopes, of mass movements :

" *Personal relationships—Here is something comparatively
solid in a world full of violence and cruelty . . . We don't
know what we are like. We can't know what other people
are like. How then can we put any trust in personal relationships, or cling to them in the gathering political storm ? In
theory we cannot. But in practice we can and do . . . I
certainly can proclaim that I believe in personal relationships.
Starting from them, I get a little order into the contemporary
chaos . . . Personal relations are despised to-day. They are
regarded as bourgeois luxuries, as products of a time of fair
weather which is now past, and we are urged to get rid of them,
and to dedicate ourselves to some movement or cause instead.
I hate the idea of causes, and if I had to choose between
betraying my country and betraying my friend, I hope I should
have the guts to betray my country . . . Love and loyalty to
an individual can run counter to the claims of the State. When
they do—down with the State, say I, which means that the
State would down me*".

Yes. No wonder some people disapprove of Mr.
Forster. Again and again through all his books there is
that upholding of personal relationships as the only firm
thing in a world of chaos and darkness. Those who hold
to these are saved ; those who betray or ignore them are
damned. It is the clearest and the most important of the
cleavages, the testing lines of division, that, as has been
often pointed out, divide his characters into saved, lost, and
struggling on the border-line. There are other dividing
lines. But these spiritual conflicts and categories concern
Mr. Forster the moralist ; I shall return to them presently.
For in commenting upon E. M. Forster, whether as
novelist, essayist or critic, one is dealing with many
separate, though inter-related, aspects of his mind.

The word " aspect " sends one to his Clark lectures on
the Novel; where at the end of the introductory chapter

we find the sentence, "The aspects selected for discussion
are seven in number : the Story ; People ; the Plot ;
Fantasy and Prophesy ; Pattern and Rhythm ". These
would do pretty well for the terms in which to consider
Mr. Forster's own work as a novelist ; though it leaves
out two important things—style, and wit.

When one says " work as a novelist ", one bears in
mind that he is, of course, not a novelist only ; he is a
sensitive literary critic, a delightful and witty essayist, a
perceptive biographer : but I have not the space for all
this, so I am concentrating on some of the many aspects
of his novels. Plot or story, then (we can take them
together, though they are not the same). We all know
that Mr. Forster said, " Yes—oh dear yes—the novel tells
a story . . . I wish that it was not so, that it could be
something different—melody, or perception of the truth,
not this low atavistic form ". And we all know too that
he is himself a most adept story-teller ; his tales are
contrived with inevitable, unforced skill, ingenuity that
conceals ingenuity ; passions spin the plot, which moves
along with swift ease through drama, melodrama,
violence, the subtleties, extravagances and delicate
relationships of human intercourse, arriving at climaxes
classic in their structure, in their suggestion of fate and
the gods, ending in quiet finales, all passion for the
moment spent, frustrated or fulfilled. From the delicate
flickering pages sudden tragedies and events spring on us
with the bland, unheralded ferocity of the larger cats
stalking their prey on noiseless feet through whispering
jungles ; yet not quite unheralded, for there have been
hints and omens to put the perceptive reader wise. The
events are never without bearing, never irrelevant ; they
are at times symbolic, they do more than weave a plot.
People drop dead without warning ; and yet we have

G

been warned. Mr. Forster has, as the Quakers put it, a
" concern " with sudden deaths. Kidnapped babies are
flung from overturned carriages and killed ; strong,
coarse young athletes go out to play football, and, quite
casually, " Gerald died that afternoon. He was broken
up in the football match ", almost as if Mr. Forster was
too tired of Gerald to endure him any longer. Rickie
Elliot, at the end of the same book, perceives his half
brother lying drunk across the rails at a level crossing :

*" Wearily he did a man's duty. There was time to raise
him up and push him into safety. It is also a man's duty to
save his own life, and therefore he tried. The train went over
his knees. He died up in Cadover, whispering ' You have
been right' to Mrs. Failing ".*

And, in "Howards End," Charles Wilcox accidentally
kills Leonard Bast, the sad young clerk. He calls at the
house . . . Charles Wilcox cries out :

*" ' Oh, is he there ? I am not surprised. I can now thrash
him within an inch of his life '.*

" ' Mrs. Wilcox ', said Leonard, ' I have done wrong '.

*" The man took him by the collar, and cried, ' Bring me a
stick '.*

*" Women were screaming. A stick, very bright, descended.
It hurt him not where it descended, but in the heart. Books fell
over him in a shower. Nothing had sense.*

*" ' Get some water ', commanded Charles, who had all
through kept very calm. He's shamming. Of course I only
used the blade. Here, carry him out into the air '.*

*" Thinking that he understood these things, Margaret obeyed
him. They laid Leonard, who was dead, on the gravel ; Helen
poured water over him ".*

As to Mrs. Wilcox, one chapter ends with her walking
out of King's Cross Station with her husband and

daughter, the next begins " The funeral was over " ;
and we learn that Mrs. Wilcox has been the funeral's
protagonist.

In " A Passage to India ", the elderly Mrs. Moore dies
suddenly in the heat of the Red Sea. But that is not
unexpected ; since for some time she has been very hot
and queer. The surprise assault, the pounce of the large
cat, in " A Passage to India ", is not death, but the attack,
or imagined attack, on Adela Quested in the caves—
that questionable, mysterious incident on which the book
revolves. That is indeed a pounce ; and the fact that we
never learn precisely what it was that pounced gives it the
sinister quality of the unknown animal—or was it a
ghost ?—that rushed into the car in which the English
are driving in the dusk. For as Mr. Forster says, " nothing
in India is identifiable, the mere asking of a question
causes it to disappear and to merge in something else ".

There is, alas, no time to elaborate the odd, delicate
balances, contrivances and evolutions of Mr. Forster's
plots. One must pass on to his people ; his characters.
And it is here that his unique quality shows itself most.
Taken on any plane, his presentment of people, in their
essence and in all the external quirks of personality, is
most delicately exact. Tones of speech, for instance.
He is perhaps the only novelist, apart from Jane Austen,
none of whose characters could, when speaking, be
confused with any others in the book. And this without
any of the obvious tricks and slogans which those whom
he calls " flat " characters in fiction fly like identifying
flags. We know his people by their voices, and the
slight small idioms of speech, as surely as if we heard
them speak. His sense of persons is so acute that every
word they say comes to us charged with their personality ; this makes the conversations in all the novels both

enchantingly amusing and absorbingly apprehensible. Unless, of course, we are like Mr. Wilcox, who " never noticed the lights and shades that exist in the greyest conversations, the finger-posts, the milestones, the illimitable views ".

Almost any fragment of conversation, trivial or serious, might be quoted with profit and pleasure. Here is Gino, the young Italian braggart in " Where Angels fear to Tread ", telling his friend in the street about his marriage to a rich Englishwoman :

" ' *But tell me more,* ' " (the friend says). " ' *She is English. That is good, very good. An English wife is very good indeed. And she is rich ?* '

" ' *Immensely rich* '.

" ' *Blonde or dark ?* '

" ' *Blonde* '.

" ' *Is it possible ?* '

" ' *It pleases me very much* ', said Gino simply. ' *If you remember, I have always desired a blonde* '. *Three or four men had collected and were listening.*

" ' *We all desire one* ', said Spiridione. ' *But you, Gino, deserve your good fortune, for you are a good son, a brave man, and a true friend, and from the very first moment I saw you I wished you well* '.

" ' *No compliments, I beg* ', said Gino, standing with his hands crossed on his chest, and a smile of pleasure on his face.

" ' *Spiridione addressed the other men, none of whom he had ever seen before. ' Is it not true ? Does not he deserve this wealthy blonde ?* '

" ' *He does deserve her* ', said all the men."

And here are Rickie Elliot and Agnes, his dreadful fiancée, discussing his short stories in a restaurant.

" ' Can't you try something longer, Rickie ? ' she said. ' I believe we're on the wrong tack. Try an out and out love story '.

" ' My notion just now ' he replied, ' is to leave the passions on the fringe '. She nodded, and tapped for the waiter . . . ' I can't soar ; I can only indicate. That's where the musicians have the pull, for music has wings, and when she says ' Tristan ', and he says ' Isolde ', you are on the heights at once. What do people mean when they call love music artificial ? '

" ' I know what they mean, though I can't exactly explain. Or couldn't you make your stories more obvious ? I don't see any harm in that. Uncle Willie floundered hopelessly. He doesn't read much, and he got muddled. I tried to explain, and then he was delighted. Of course, to write down to the public would be quite another thing and horrible. You have certain ideas, and you must express them. But couldn't you express them more clearly ? '

" ' You see— ' He got no further than ' you see '.

" ' The soul and the body. The soul's what matters ', said Agnes, and tapped for the waiter again. He looked at her admiringly, but felt that she was not a perfect critic. Perhaps she was too perfect for a critic ".

I suppose Mr. Forster could write a play ; but perhaps not ; perhaps his is too delicate an art, and depends too much on the expression of his own slant, to subsist wholly on conversation and plot. But what a cast he has : what a collection of superbly alive elderly ladies, (scarcely any old gentlemen—why not ?) young men, young women, of all classes, all races, all tempers, an infinite variety of idioms, hearts and minds.

This sensitiveness to character and personality would naturally lead to a strong emphasis on personal relationships. The real tragedies in Mr. Forster's novels are not the sudden deaths, but the failures in human relationships, the betrayals, the hates, the inability to understand. And this brings us to the aspect he has called " Prophesy " ; or call it if you like the moral thesis, the mystical element, that underlies and runs through all his work, below the shimmering façade of wit, poetry and style, classing the figures in his exquisitely differentiated gallery as " saved " or " lost ", as typifying reality or sham, primitive honest naturalness or stifling pretentious convention, but above all dividing them into those who like their fellows and those who don't, those to whom personal relations are real and those to whom they are not. The attitude of the Wilcoxes, the successful business men, is one of hard, vulgar, contemptuous, some critics have said exaggerated, suspicion—something like that of the English towards the Indians in " A Passage to India ". In this book indeed the issue of personal relations is extended, and merged in the racial issue. Personal friendship is an irrelevant affirmation in a huge negation ; nothing can be built on it. Yet there remains kindness, " more kindness, and even after that more kindness. I assure you ", says Aziz, the young Moslem, " I assure you it is the only hope. We can't build up India except on what we feel ".

But in the early novels, and in the short stories, the battle is waged between the vivid and the dull ; the happy savage against the cultured snob ; natural human passion against the restraints of convention ; the vivid moment against the long littleness of life. The fight is to the death ; sometimes one side wins, sometimes the other. The forces of life are represented by the simple and happy young, by the moment of ecstasy, by the honest and the serious ; sometimes by the gay civilization of Italy, sometimes by the wide bucolic spaces of

Wiltshire, always by Cambridge, whose culture and companionships might be called a recurrent motif, even where only implicit. The forces of darkness are symbolized by the suburban drabness of Sawston, by proprieties, repressions and lies.

Those, if there are any, who think of this dealer in desperate conflicts, salvation and damnation, as a cosy purveyor of bourgeois tea-table amenities, have let themselves be misled by the siren appeal of charm, style and humour that pervades his work ; they call it playfulness, archness, even whimsicality, and demand a grim novel, possibly about miners. But, though not (so far) about miners, Mr. Forster's novels *are* grim in their implications ; they have an almost Dante-esque concern with hell, only the hell is in the present. He would endorse Sir Thomas Browne's " Surely though we place Hell under the earth, the Devil's walk and purlue is about it. The heart of man is the place the devils dwell in. I feel sometimes a Hell within myself . . ." For Mr. Forster is a mystic. In his early short stories, he was apt to play with supernatural beings and events—fauns, dryads and the god Pan leapt from their brakes and subverted the lives of the human beings. Later he kept them more in their thickets, but some of the human beings have many of their attributes. Fantasy gave place to poetry. For the poet has always been a prominent partner in his work. Whatever critics may say, for instance, of " A Passage to India ", as a story, a study of a problem, a study of races and of people, it must live for its sheer beauty. The words, the precise, clear detail, so unexpected, so unliterary, have the qualities of the poet's or artist's direct vision. One could say the same of the other books : but in this the beauty, the poetic content, reaches new heights. One could quote passage after passage . . .

What one can't illustrate by quoting, is the rhythm and pattern that runs through all the novels, like the pattern that connects a symphony ; it is perhaps allied to Mr. Forster's interest in music. One can best express it by saying that nothing that happens in the novels is irrelevant, or outside the stream of logic and consequence ; it all connects. Nor will quoting fragments illustrate style, or, in Mr. Forster's case, even his pervasive wit, for this doesn't consist of epigrams or jokes ; it is inherent in his view of his characters and of life. But take the conversation in " A Passage to India " between the new arrival, Adela Quested, and the ladies at the English club. Adela has been expressing her desire to see Indians :

" ' *As if one could avoid seeing them* ' *sighed Mrs. Lesley.*
" ' *I've avoided* ' *said Miss Quested.* ' *Excepting my own servant, I've scarcely spoken to an Indian since landing* '.
" ' *Oh, lucky you* '.
" ' *But I want to see them* '.
" *She became the centre of an amused group of ladies. One said,* ' *Wanting to see Indians. How new that sounds !* ' *Another,* ' *Natives ! Why, fancy !* ' *A third, more serious, said,* ' *Let me explain. Natives don't respect one any more after meeting one, you see* '.
" ' *That occurs after so many meetings* '.
" *But the lady, entirely stupid and friendly, continued* . . ."

Delightful to read ; acutely exact in observation. But " A Passage to India ", though on a larger scale, and though it has had the widest appeal, and in spite of its high poetic quality and magnificent scope, is not, to my mind, the best of the novels. I put higher myself the three commentaries on then contemporary life that appeared from thirty to forty years ago—and have with the years taken on a delicate period flavour—" The

Longest Journey ", " A Room with a View ", and
" Howards End "—I think the best and richest of all
. . . The *then* contemporary life ; it is our loss that
our present troubled age lacks this unequalled chronicler.
One can but hope . . .

GEORGE ORWELL

by V. S. PRITCHETT

WHEN PEOPLE speak of the English tradition, the traditional English things and the traditional Englishman —when they use these words they usually mean something rich, sedate, and warmly coloured by a wise and romantic respect for the past. The word " conservative " sums up the general implication. But, a moment's reflection shows what a lopsided view of tradition this is. It is just as true to think of the English tradition as the tradition of rebellion. The English rebel, sometimes bleak, sometimes flamboyant and fanatical, always unflagging, unbendable and individual is a constant figure in our life.

Take names at random : Milton, Defoe, Cobbett, John Stuart Mill and Wells, and dozens more ; the spirit of rebellion, non-conformity and attack stands out in them. They are, in their degrees, non-cooperators. They see the world as a series of tyrannous brick walls against which they are impelled to bash their heads ; sometimes they damage themselves, sometimes they knock the wall down and then we are grateful to them ; sometimes there was no wall there and they fall flat on their faces with surprise. The English rebels delight in public abuse. They are not deterred by accepted loyalties. They hate the acquiescent mind, and when their enemies come to know them and grapple with them, it is to discover how English they are. At the heart of every English rebel is a conservative : they are simply the growing points of society.

I am going to speak about one of the younger generation of living writers—George Orwell, who continues our tradition of rebellion. And I would like to say again, that without it, life in England would be even less endurable for the majority of people, than it is.

Orwell is the odd man out in English writing. He has gone his own way entirely. He is the most original of his contemporaries. He might be described as a writer who has " gone native " in his own country. He belongs to no group, he joins no side ; if he dallies with the idea, he turns out to be a liability to his party. He is on his own. But not flamboyantly, not theatrically, not, for example, like Shaw or Cunningham Graham. George Orwell is rashly, almost bleakly, almost colourlessly and uncomfortably, on his own, but he does not stand still. His sincerity, his honesty give his writing its distinguishing quality : dramatic speed of movement and startling changes of subject.

What a variety there is in Orwell's books ! When he left Eton, Orwell went out to Burma as a police officer, and the first thing I read of his—it appeared in " New Writing "—was a remarkable report of a young police officer going out to shoot a rogue elephant. It was more than an incident in big game shooting : it was also an essay in political psychology. And yet the moment of the elephant's death is described as by someone who liked words and images for their own sake ; and both the originality and seriousness of the point of view and

the excellence of the writing showed one that Orwell
had the first quality that marks the superior writer—
the quality I call " the dilatory eye ". The outstanding
writers do not rush on ; they stop to gaze and absorb :

" *When I pulled the trigger I did not hear the bang or feel
the kick—one never does when a shot goes home—but I heard
the devilish roar of glee that went up from the crowd. In that
instant, in too short a time, one would have thought, even for
the bullet to get there, a mysterious, terrible change had come
over the elephant. He neither stirred nor fell, but every line
of his body had altered. He looked suddenly stricken, shrunken,
immensely old, as though the frightful impact of the bullet had
paralysed him without knocking him down. At last, after
what seemed a long time—it might have been five seconds,
I say,—he sagged flabbily to his knees. His mouth slobbered.
An enormous senility seemed to have settled upon him. One
could have imagined him thousands of years old. I fired again
into the same spot. At the second shot he did not collapse but
climbed with desperate slowness to his feet and stood weakly
upright, with his legs sagging and head drooping. I fired a
third time. That was the shot that did for him. You could see
the agony of it jolt his whole body and knock the last remnant
of strength from his legs. But in falling he seemed for a
moment to rise, for as his hind legs collapsed beneath him he
seemed to tower upwards like a huge rock toppling, his trunk
reaching skyward like a tree. He trumpeted, for the first and
only time. And then down he came, his belly towards me,
with a crash that seemed to shake the ground even where I lay* ".

Orwell's revolt might have been dreary to the reader,
but for the consuming curiosity of his eye. I do not
think there is any living writer so absorbedly, so
enquiringly interested in gregarious life; and so unlikely
to conform to other peoples' view of it. Orwell left

the Burma police because he turned against British rule in that country ; and wrote a scathing and vivid novel with the amusingly old-fashioned title of " Burmese Days " : many an Anglo-Indian must have thought it a collection out of " Blackwoods " and must have had a shock when he read it. Orwell's social knowledge of the Burmese was intricate ; his pictures of the white man have a contempt mingled with pity. On the other hand the Burmese are not pictured as saints. Orwell is in fact not the usual minority man who turns against the British Empire and who makes heroes of the oppressed simply because they are oppressed. Orwell is far subtler and far more honest than that. He is really an active moralist, a preacher who sees that oppression creates hypocrisy, and that hypocrisy corrupts. He scents the decay in civilisation with an almost fanatical nose. He detests the decay yet he has too much detachment to be a fanatic. There is a note of flat tiredness too, a note of the wearied saint. This Burmese novel is written on the raw ; its realm is as distinct as anything in Kipling or E. M. Forster. It used to be said after the fall of Singapore that the novels of Somerset Maugham had indirectly prophesied it ; Orwell went further than Maugham ; Orwell's prophecy was savage and direct. And yet, all the time he is interested, more and more absorbed by the dejection of the life he describes. And he writes with a bitter humour and wit, punctuated by sudden bouts of sympathy and pity for the people he has attacked.

Then there is a thwarted poet in Orwell, who comes out in one or two of the jungle descriptions in " Burmese Days ". The taste for squalour and corruption in contemporary writing is important because it shows how responsive the most sensitive and honourable writers

have been to the breakdown of the defences of their
culture. Revolution and the desire for justice bring the
dirty and the shabby to the top : beautiful things recede,
sink away, are almost forgotten unless a chance
experience recalls them.

" *There was a stirring high up in the peepul tree, and a
bubbling noise like pots boiling. A flock of green pigeons were
up there, eating the berries. Flory gazed up into the great
green dome of the tree, trying to distinguish the birds ; they
were invisible, they matched the leaves so perfectly, and yet the
whole tree was alive with them, shimmering, as though the
ghosts of birds were shaking it.*

" *Flo rested herself against the roots and growled up at the
invisible creatures. Then a single green pigeon fluttered down
and perched on a lower branch. It did not know that it was
being watched. It was a tender thing, smaller than a tame
dove, with jade-green back as smooth as velvet, and neck and
breast of iridescent colours. Its legs were like the pink wax
that dentists use.*

" *The pigeon rocked itself backwards and forwards on the
bough, swelling out its breast feathers and laying its coralline
beak upon them. A pang went through Flory. Alone, alone,
the bitterness of being alone ! So often like this, in lonely
places in the forest, he would come upon something—bird,
flower, tree—beautiful beyond all words, if there had been a
soul with whom to share it. Beauty is meaningless until it is
shared.*

" *If he had one person, just one, to halve his loneliness !
Suddenly the pigeon saw the man and dog below, sprang into
the air and dashed away swift as a bullet, with a rattle of
wings. One does not often see green pigeons so closely when
they are alive. They are high-flying birds, living in the
treetops, and they do not come to the ground, or only to drink.
When one shoots them, if they are not killed outright, they*

*cling to the branch until they die, and drop long after one has
given up waiting and gone away*".

I've just noticed that my two quotations have been
about animals. I suppose that Orwell prefers animals to
human beings. Anyway, he prefers the outcast human
being. . . .From the sahib Orwell turned to the vagrant.
He hated being the ruler, he wanted to be (for a while)
the victim and the ruled.

To be down and out in Europe was like being some
kinds of Burmese, so he wrote "Down and Out in Paris
and London", a book describing his experiences of
poverty and semi-starvation in the slums of Paris and the
doss houses of London. Here his dominant quality as a
writer emerges. He is a documentary writer, a kind of
social anthropoligist. What is starvation like ? What
is the day of a starving man, a tramp, a hawker, any
casual labourer ? 15,000 men slept in poor hostels every
night in London, at the time of Orwell's book. I don't
know what the figures are now. Who are these people,
why are they there ? What are the characters of those
who live below the poverty line ?

"The Road to Wigan Pier" does the same thing for
the life of the mean shop and lodging house. Who are
these unwashed, semi-illiterates, who scrape a living
together and who are outside the main social categories ?
The nature of Orwell's writing becomes clearer. He is
not a writer about the organised, self-improving masses :
he is a connoisseur of the outcast.

But some middle class people are just as much outcasts
as the inhabitants of the doss house or the dying shop—
I ought to say these books were written during the
unemployment period—and such an outcast is the chief
figure in "The Vicar's Daughter".

The book is a novel, and the heroine is an outcast because she has been totally unfitted by her mean, sheltered, pious life, to cope with life in the open when, through loss of memory, she comes against it. Once more Orwell is the anthropologist. What a thin veil separates the " nice " from the distinctly "nasty" ! The book was an episodic novel, a kind of dramatised social tract.

Orwell is really a kind of English traveller, and when the Spanish war started, he became a travelling revolutionary, a soldier. He fought for the Republicans in Catalonia. And here his political type appeared. He joined the minority ; the dissident communist group, known as the P.O.U.M. P.O.U.M. was persecuted and at last attacked by the orthodox Communists and in " Homage to Catalonia " Orwell wrote his protest against what seemed to him a cynical betrayal. And from that time onward he has become the passionate enemy of Stalinist Russia, which he satirised with acid humour in a fable about farm animals called " Animal Farm ". Bitter and destructive as this fable is—by far the most destructive criticism that has yet appeared on Soviet Russia—it is warm, tragic and humane. There is a fruitful undercurrent of homely sanity at the bottom of all Orwell's work, a kind of instinct for checking the intellect when it is tempted to leap into the casuistries by which the intellectual in our time has dodged ordinary human decency. But this has not prevented Orwell from becoming, as time goes by, more and more the rebel pamphleteer, the minority man, spoiling for trouble. There has been only one interlude in this pamphleteering : a collection of critical essays on literary subjects. Essays on Kipling and Dickens above all ; and then some extraordinarily original and penetrating analyses of boys' papers and popular literature—things like " No Orchids for Miss Blandish " and P. G. Wodehouse. Orwell has become the first critic of real popular commercial culture.

No other English writer has entered this uncouth and fertile field ; no one has indeed applied political anthropology so fruitfully to popular literature. His approach owes a great deal to Marxism.

That then, is a rapid survey of the ground over which Orwell travels, with astonishing and exclusive certainty about what he is after. He is searching for the sinister fact, the hushed up tendency ; he is looking for accepted legends to expose.

You say "I am sorry for the poor" ; Orwell says " You are sorry you have to be sorry about the poor. Stripped to essentials what you mean is that you're sitting pretty and you don't give a damn ". You say, " Boys' books are just healthy amusement for the young ". Orwell says, " Boys' books are social propoganda, expressly designed by a hundred and one discreet touches, to create boys who are malleable to the ruling interest ". You say, " Gangster books are harmless escapism ". Orwell says, " Gangster books disclose the Fascist tendency of society, the worship of what Fascists and Communists called " Political realism " and power for its own sake ". He doesn't say these things as crudely as I have said them, he says them clearly, but with great subtlety. The thing he leaves out, you will have already noticed is the aesthetic question. A bad book means as much, for his purpose as a good one. He is not interested in what makes books good ; but in the propaganda they inculcate. He subscribes to Trotsky's doctrine—one that seems to me, I must confess, ultimately meaningless ; that all art is propaganda. I am sure that Orwell knows

H

what an irrelevance this doctrine is ; he would urge that in revolutionary times like ours, the aesthetic question, what makes a good book and how we recognise it, is irrelevant. The value of his point of view is that it traces literature back to its sources in life : the weakness is that literature has equally important sources in literature, in the history and nature of the imagination.

But against this revolutionary attitude of Orwell's which sounds so drastic, must be put his response to honesty and kindness. Orwell's enemy is the world of 1910, Imperialistic England of that time ; yet that is the period to which he returns when he considers the naked horrors of today. The romantic snobbery of Wodehouse seems innocent compared to the " realistic " Fascist stuff of today. Kipling's Imperialism had at least the respect for law. With all its brutal defects, it had a sense of responsibility, a knowledge of the necessity of governing.

Dickens was a " softy ", a typical *petit bourgeois* of the commercial merchant classes—(how he squirms away from fights and soldiers, and what a little prig and snob he is !) And yet, why has the world loved his books ? For a quality, says Mr. Orwell, that has almost disappeared from our ordinary vocabulary, and especially from the world's political vocabulary : for Dickens believed in the great popular values—decency, ordinary kindness and mercy.

Orwell's essay on Dickens is the best thing he has ever written, and this brings me to my last point. Orwell's writing has a soldierly bleakness and greyness ; it moves rapidly, clearly, simply, full of quick asides, rash assertions, comfortless afterthoughts, like cold water. Except for the sound of his own arguing voice in his prose— which is what gives it life—his style is a neutral style. The rain falleth upon the just and upon the unjust—but in

Orwell none falls on the just. Indeed there are no just men. And yet—the decent. There are the decent. At the back of Orwell's mind there are always the decent. And that is what makes him so English, so uncompromisingly English for all his Marxism. Fags, fried fish shops, hop pickers, shop keepers, glum people with bad accents, the common crowd, which can turn so ugly, but also relapses into niceness—the vulgar England of the worst advertisements, which bears no intellectual or aesthetic examination, swarms in his book and sets their whole atmosphere. His pictures of lower middle class life recall those of Wells—with the important difference that Wells wrote from the inside and Orwell, the educated outcast, writes from the outside. Rebel and diehard—in the English fashion—that is Orwell, who has a reckless ironical leaning towards all that arouses indignation and dismay. He is the most honest writer of our time.

WALTER DE LA MARE

by DYLAN THOMAS

" WHAT I SAY IS, keep on this side of the tomb as long as you can. Don't meddle with that hole. Why? Because while some fine day you will have to go down into it, you can never be quite sure while you are here what mayn't come back out of it.

" ' There'll be no partings there—I have heard them trolling that out in their chapels like missel-thrushes in the spring. They seem to forget there may be some mighty unpleasant meetings. And what about the further shore? It's my belief there's some kind of a ferry plying on that river. And coming back depends on what you want to come back for".

So an old, smallish man, muffled in a very respectable greatcoat at least two sizes too large for him, mutters in a dark corner of the firelit station waiting-room in Walter de la Mare's uneasy story, " Crewe ".

How many of the nasty hosts, from the other side of the razor's edge, from the wrong room, from the chocka-block grave, from the trespassing hereafter, from the sly holes, crawl over and into the seedy waiting-rooms, the creeping railway carriages, the gas-lamped late Victorian teashops the colour of stewed tea, where down-at-soul strangers contrive their tales and, drop by drop, leak out the shadows of their grey or black, forlorn, and vaguely infernal secrets ! The ghosts of Mr. de la Mare, though they reek and scamper, and, in old houses at the proper bad hours, are heard sometimes at their infectious business, are not for you to see. But there is no assurance that they do not see *you*. They are but distant relatives of Dr. M. R. James's all-too-visible haunters, and hardly on curdling terms with them. Remember, in Dr. James :

" . . . *the personage in the empty bed who, with a sudden smooth motion, slipped from the bed and at last, moving into the area of light, and facing the window, revealed a horrible, an intensely horrible, face of crumpled linen* ".

And the two rent and desolate wailing children of " Lost Hearts " ; and Canon Alboric's spider :

" *Pale, dusty skin, covering nothing but bones and tendons of appalling strength ; coarse black hairs, longer than ever grew on a human hand ; nails rising from the ends of the fingers and curving sharply down and forward, grey, horny, and wrinkled* ".

And the " man " in " A School Story " :

" . . . ' *he was sitting or kneeling on Sampson's window-sill, and looking in, and I thought he was beckoning*'.
" ' *What sort of a man ?* '
" ' *I don't know, but I can tell you one thing—he was beastly thin ; and he looked as if he was wet all over ; and . . . I'm not at all sure that he was alive.*' "

And then remember, in Mr. de la Mare, the scarecrow that suddenly appears in a cornfield behind a house where lately a man has hanged himself.

" ' *Does the air round the scarecrow strike you as funny at all ?* ' I asked him. ' *Out of the way funny—quivering, in a manner of speaking ?* '

" ' *That's the heat* ', *he said, but his lip trembled* ".

And the shocking, halucinatory mask of face and head lying on Mr. Bloom's pillow. And the polluted, invisible presences that seep through the charnel-house of Seaton's bloated and grave-emptying Aunt : " *the lightest of footfalls, sounds as faint as the vanishing remembrance of voices in a dream* ".

Here in this house, and in all the other •drenched, death-storied houses, down whose corridors and stair-cases the past hisses, and in whose great mirrors you see behind you a corridor of hinted faces, and in whose lofty beds you share your sheets and nightmare with an intangible, shifted fellow or the sibilant echo of a sound you wish had never been made, most things that happen are ordinary, or very nearly ordinary, and vile. These are houses suspended in time ; and timelessness erupts in them.

Listen to what Mr. de la Mare says, in his " Pleasures and Speculations " about Hans Andersen :

" *Life then seemed to him a play of phantasms, as it often does to a child of a solitary, moody, or conscientious disposition, confronted with the amazingly real. But it was a play of phantasms with sinister shadows. A deft-fingered old gentleman lived in a madhouse close by. On the only occasion when they met he addressed his grandson as* ' *they* '. *Two prisoners waited on the child at table when he dined one day in the neighbouring jail. He impressed and alarmed the old women in the workhouse with a fantastic description of their insides. He peered in one morning on a sweet-voiced naked lunatic in her cell, who clawed at her visitor through a hole in the door* ".

Mr. de la Mare's *first* world of childhood is as " phantas-mal " and " solitary " as Hans Andersen's, but rarely so cruel—or so alive. Though on first reading or hearing, the deeper and wider meaning behind these words about Andersen might seem well to apply to de la Mare himself, soon we grow to know that a huge mythological distance separates that world where Kay and Gerda breathe for ever, and that in which the child-alone of de la Mare's tall tales go about their dreams, loves ,and surprises. The country whose habitations, whose great sleepy meadows of March mornings, blue and tumultuous and bleak, far away cold towers and pinnacles, whether of clouds or hills, valleys and spelled woods, grey-green dells, mistletoed and mustard-seeded avenues, that the children of his earliest stories people, infest, and to high music, moon, glide, and meander through, is a country of *books*. Hans Andersen's characters move in a magic that was not, beforehand, composed, pictured, or written down, but is created, there and then, by their lovely motion, and for themselves to inhabit. But in, for example, " Henry Brocken ", the first of de la Mare's long tales, the world through which the beguiled boy wanders on his mild Rosinanta is made of the trees and climates moors, mornings and evenings, groves, hills, suns, stars, and gardens, of written, remembered words, of Bunyan's allegory and Swift's satire, of the poetry of Wordsworth, Herrick, Shakespeare, Poe, and Keats. Here enamoured Henry Brocken, in the library-country, roving deep in the coils of the necromantic ball, meets Lucy Gray, Jane Eyre, Julia, Electra, Dianame, Anthea, Nick Bottom, the Sleeping Beauty, Gulliver, La Belle Dame Sans Merci, Annabel Lee. But, overdecorated, remote, rooted in " reverie " (that favourite woollen-headed word), the adventure is all shades. Henry Brocken is a bookish and starry-eyed mood on a borrowed horse. The fabled earth is cloud. Clouds are reflections and echoes of sea-waves that rhyme with other words. Rarely just pretty or arch, the way of the story is too often sadly sweet and singlenoted. Though Bottom of the dream is a pastoral man, the chapter about him is as country-woven as the bottom of a river seen through floating Desdemona weed painted by Burne-Jones : though not so solid. There is a fine phrase in " Pleasures and Speculations " which could, in a way, help to describe the story.

" *A silver-fish, to some fancies, has a touch of magic. It is nocturnal ; it feeds on starch ; it is acutely silent* ".

But as Mr. de la Mare went on writing, his children went on growing. They did not grow into youths, but into children. They lost that lorn and dewy wonder, and when they moved, though always on odd errands, they did not rustle like the pages of an old book turned in a lamplit brown study by a wan, near-tenuous, but inky hand. " Homesick ", " forlorn ", " lost ", and " silent " these words were used less often, though the nostalgia for the " mournful gaiety " of the past, the loneliness, the silence, and the delirium, still were there. In an essay called, " A Book of Words ", written years after these first childhood stories, he writes :

" *I once knew a child less than three years old whose 'f's' were all 's's'. ' Oh, mummy ', he cried one fine morning on seeing some dead rabbits hanging up in a fishmonger's shop, ' look at those sunny surry sish ' ".*

It was through Mr. de la Mare's perception of the very *natural* oddity and immediacy of childhood—as seen, so much later, in that casual anecdote—that a story like " The Almond Tree " emerged, most movingly, out of the tapestried and *unnatural* " farness " of Henry Brocken.

Nicholas in " The Almond Tree " is, in Mr. Forrest Reid's words, " the first of a line of strange, wayward, intelligent, dangerously sensitive, infinitely alive small boys ". In later stories, his name changes, he is older or younger, sadder or gayer, more darkly cunning or more coldly innocent, now embroiled and tangled in briary thickets of love, now critical and aloof, faintly smiling, in fear and evil occurrences ; but always his eyes are the same. It is through these eyes we see the astonishing systems, the unpredictable order, of life on the edge of its answer or quivering on a poisonous threshold.

Children, Mr. de la Mare writes in his essay on Hans Andersen :

" . . . *do not gape at their own innocence, or marvel at imaginations as natural to them as spectacles on an elderly nose, or sit cherubically smiling at themselves amid their trailing clouds of glory. They dwell and flourish in their own natures, preternaturally practical and crafty pygmies in the world of dull tyrannical tyrants into which it has pleased God to call them* ".

Only on slight occasions do Mr. de la Mare's children come into contact with each other. We see them, nearly always, in their relation to abnormal men and women. And, of his children, it is only the small boys who become real The little girls live in a distant, and more fragile past.

A " *more* fragile " past ; for he is loyal, always, to old Ways and Days, old houses, regions, customs, scents, and colours. His children loiter, wonder, and perceive, his men and women suffer, love, and are haunted, his weathers happen, his dead-behind-the-wainscot blow and scamper, in a time and place that was before he was born. The life of his countryside is that which his mother remembered, hearing *her* mother tell of, and of which she told him when he was a child. His imagined memories of childhood are all of a timeless past before his own :

" *The house of my first remembrance, the house that to my last hour on earth will seem home to me, stood in a small green hollow on the verge of a wide heath. Its five upper windows faced far eastwards towards the weather-cocked tower of a village which rambled down the steep inclination of a hill. And walking in its green old garden . . . you could see in the evening the standing fields of corn and the dark furrows where the evening star was stationed, and a little to the south, upon a crest, a rambling wood of fir trees and bracken. . . Here passed by, to the singing of the lark, and the lamentation of autumn wind and rain, those first long nine of all these heaped-up inextricable years. Even now, my heart leaps up with longing to see again with those untutored eyes the lofty clouds of evening ; to hear again as then I heard it the two small notes of the yellow-hammer piping from his green spray. I remember every room of the old house, the steep stairs, the cool apple-scented pantry ; I remember the cobbles by the scullery, the well, my old dead raven, the bleak and whistling elms ; but best of all I remember the unmeasured splendour of the heath, with its gorse, and its deep canopy of sunny air, the haven of every wild bird of the morning* ".

In " Miss Duveen ", the child-of-all the stories meets, for the first time, the elderly abnormal lady—on rather unpleasantly more than a nodding acquaintance with her invisible neighbours—who is later to appear under several names and disguises, as evil-favoured Aunt Charlotte and ghastly Seaton's Aunt. And as the original " lady-in-waiting ", Miss Duveen is more obviously cracked and less perilous than her tribal sisters-to-be ;

she is almost gross in her communion with the mad dead. As Miss Seaton, in the later story, she is made subtle ; ponderous, sabbath-and-bombazine-black respectability keeps apparent insanity *out :* and *in* come the legions, ravers and dwergers, with gibberish and stinking eyes.

Miss Duveen is the neighbour of the child ; the backs of their gardens meet, they become acquainted.

" ' *Ah,* ' *she said,* . . . ' *So this is the young gentleman, the bold, gallant young gentleman. And what might be his name ? '*

" *I replied rather distantly that my name was Arthur.*

" ' *Arthur, to be sure ! ' she repeated with extraordinary geniality, and again,* ' *Arthur* ', *as if in the strictest confidence.*

" ' *I know you, Arthur, very well indeed. I have looked, I have watched ; and now, please God, we need never be estranged* ' . . . *She gathered up her tiny countenance once more into an incredible grimace of friendliness ; and I smiled as amicably as I could in return. There was a pause in this one-sided conversation. She seemed to be listening, and her lips moved, though I caught no sound. In my uneasiness I was just about to turn stealthily away, when she poked forward again.*

" ' *Yes, yes, I know you quite intimately, Arthur. We have met* here '. *She tapped her rounded forehead.* ' *You might not suppose it, too ; but I have eyes like a lynx. It is no exaggeration, I assure you—I assure everybody. And now what friends we will be ! At times* ', *she stepped out of her hiding-place and stood in curious dignity beside the water, her hands folded in front of her on her black pleated silk apron—* ' *at times, dear child, I long for company—earthly company* '. *She glanced furtively about her.* ' *But I must restrain my longings ; and you will, of course, understand that I do not complain* . . .

" ' *I, you know* ', *she said suddenly, raising her little piercing eyes to mine,* ' *I am Miss Duveen, that's not, they say, quite the thing here* '. *She tapped her small forehead again beneath its two sleek curves of greying hair, and made a long narrow mouth at me.* ' *Though, of course* ', *she added,* ' *we do not tell* her *so. No !* '

" *And I, too, nodded my head in instinctive and absorbed imitation. Miss Duveen laughed gaily.* ' *He understands, he understands !* ' *she cried, as if to many listeners.* ' *Oh, what a joy it is in this world, Arthur, to be understood* ' ".

Intriguing, grotesque, pathetic lady, victim of love, in love again—with a child.

But Miss Seaton is vindictively *out* of love with *all* the living, and unmentionably attached to the departed whom she will not let lie. Seaton, a twisted, furtive boy, positive of his eventual undoing, brings a schoolfriend home for the half-term holiday to his aunt's house. The tadpole pond in the garden is *swarming* with the most horrible, slimy creatures ; but in the high house behind its huge sycamore, only the Aunt awaits the boys.

" *We were approaching the house when Seaton suddenly came to a standstill. Indeed, I have always had the impression that he plucked at my sleeve. Something, at least, seemed to catch me back, as it were, as he cried :* ' *Look out, there she is !* '

" *She was standing at an upper window which opened wide on a hinge, and at first sight she looked an excessively tall and overwhelming figure. This, however, was mainly because the window reached all but to the floor of her bedroom. She was in reality rather an under-sized woman, in spite of her long face and big head. She must have stood, I think, unusually still, with eyes fixed on us, though this impression may be due to Seaton's sudden warning and to my consciousness*

*of the cautious and subdued air that had fallen on him at sight of
her. I know that without the least reason in the world I felt
a kind of guiltiness, as if I had been " caught. " There was
a silvery star pattern sprinkled on her black silk dress, and even
from the ground I could see the immense coils of her hair and
the rings on her left hand which was held fingering the small
jet buttons of her bodice. She watched our united advance
without stirring, until, imperceptibly, her eyes raised and lost
themselves in the distance, so that it was out of an assumed
reverie that she appeared suddenly to awaken to our presence
beneath her when we drew close to the house ".*

Mr. de la Mare's stories first appeared about 1900. One
of the first reviewers to recognise his awakening genius
was Francis Thompson. And last year, at the end of a
lovely poem called " A Portrait ", he wrote of himself :

" *A foolish fond old man, his bed-time nigh,*
Who still at western window stays to win
A transient respite from the latening sky,
And scarce can bear it when the Sun goes in ".

Through all those intermediary years he has written
long and short stories, for children, about children, for
grown men and dead men, for the unborn, for a liveli-
hood, for nothing, for the best reward, through innocence
and with wide and deep skill, for pleasure, for fun, from
suffering, and for himself. We have looked only at a
very few aspects of Walter de la Mare's work. Nothing
has been said, for example, of " The Return ", " The
Memoirs of A Midget ", " All Hallows ", " A Recluse ",
" Missing ", " Miss Jemima ", " The Creatures ", " An
Ideal Craftsman ", and of the strange and beautiful story
I like best, the story called " At First Sight ".

How many other important points have been
neglected ! For example, his influences ? . . . Sir

Thomas Browne, de Quincey, Ecclesiastes, Henry James, Emily Brontë, Stevenson, Poe, Traherne—these perhaps are some of them. And, in later life, Julian Green.

And his style ? . . . It is his stories. At the very beginning, he was fond, I think, of a rather flowery verbosity ; he used a lot of clichés, but they were always the right ones.

There was the suggestion of something, even in a young man, old-maidenish about his attitude to the love of men for women. Country terror was a little cosy, so that you felt not that something nasty had happened in the woodshed but that there were quite hellish goings on among the woolbaskets in the parlour.

The period and place about which he writes ? Somewhere in the Southern Counties, say anywhere after 1830 . . . and just before the after-life.

In his more mature dramatic stories about grown-up human relationships, he often used a convoluted monologue-manner that occasionally suggested the ghost of a landbound Conrad talking from behind a pot of ferns. A fault of the prose-style, always avoided in the verse, was a gravy-like thickening of texture. And his elaborate language, fuller than ever of artifice and allusion when it was seemingly simple, did not suit, to my mind, the more-or-less straightforward, or the grotesque fairy-story. His *real* fairies are as endearing as Dracula.

And his subject, always, is the imminence of spiritual danger. Only rarely does Mr. de la Mare himself obtrude, avuncularly, into those fantasies that tremble on the razor's edge, at the door of the wrong room, on the rim of the chockablock grave. " At First Sight " is, to me, one of the best stories in English. But I shall end with a passage from a far earlier story : " The Creatures".

" You stand, you sit, or lie prone on its bud-starred heights, and look down ; the green, dispersed, treeless landscape spreads beneath you, with its hollows and mounded slopes, clustering farmstead, and scatter of village, all motionless under the vast wash of sun and blue, like the drop-scene of some enchanted playhouse centuries old. So, too, the visionary bird-haunted headlands, veiled faintly in a mist of reality above their broken stones and the enormous saucer of the sea.

" You cannot guess what you may chance upon, or whom. Bells clash, boom, and quarrel hollowly on the edge of darkness in those breakers. Voices waver across the fainter winds. The birds cry in a tongue unknown yet not unfamiliar. The sky is the hawks' and the stars'."

ALDOUS HUXLEY

by PETER QUENNELL

ALDOUS HUXLEY is an imposing subject—there can be no mistake about it. Years ago one might have hoped to skirmish around his achievement in a few enthusiastic or denigratory paragraphs. But today his collected works are formidable, judged by their bulk alone. Consider his score. Since 1920 he has published twenty-nine volumes : seven novels, twelve collections of essays and belles lettres, five volumes of short stories, two books of verse, one drama, one biography, one philosophical and religious treatise. Well, to this Himalayan mass of works I see three separate lines of approach that might profitably be followed.

One might discuss the writer as a social phenomenon, a characteristic product of the between-war period. One might examine his spiritual progress and seek to show how he has graduated from intellectual scepticism to religious mysticism. Lastly—which is what I propose to do—one might attempt to trace the development of a literary artist who, whether you like or dislike his work, must certainly be classed among the most gifted and versatile of the present generation.

Let us look back to 1920. I doubt if any other modern writer has started his career with finer intellectual

equipment, a more abundant air of promise. A common
friend, who knew him at Oxford, has told me of the
surprise, envy, confusion experienced by his fellow
undergraduates when, at the weekly tutorial, they heard
him read aloud his essays. The mature Huxley had
already taken shape. It was all there—the erudition, the
gift of language, the love of paradox, together with that
invaluable knack of discovering stimulating parallels,
provocative analogies, between completely different
subjects. His first books were strikingly accomplished.
" Leda ", a book of verse, and " Limbo ", a collection
of admirable short stories, were published in 1920, when
their author was twenty-six. A year later came " Crome
Yellow ", a novel in the style of Peacock, satirical,
cynical, poetic—not perhaps an " important " book in
the more ponderous sense of the adjective, but a book
that I can still re-read—indeed, have often re-read—with
very great enjoyment.

But to see " Crome Yellow " in proper perspective
we must remember the state of the English novel when
Huxley was a young man. Neither James Joyce nor
Virginia Woolf was as yet much in evidence. "Ulysses",
that magnificent deformity, and " Jacob's Room ", that
graceful changeling, were not presented to the public till
1922 ; and it was some time before either Joyce or
Woolf began to exert a decisive influence upon their
fellow writers.

Wells and Bennett were still predominant. They
carried on the tradition of the 19th century realistic
novel, with its accurate pictures of social life, its solid
well-constructed plot, its matter-of-fact dialogue. Very
different—and by comparison extremely refreshing—
were the qualities of " Crome Yellow ". Whereas
novelists like Wells laboured under the burden of ideas,

I

Aldous Huxley juggled with them. The book is full of
conversation, and the talk ranges to and fro in a manner
at once light and learned, penetrative and yet poetic,
reaching no definite conclusion but constantly illuminat-
ing the page with a flash of wit or insight. Most of the
characters are loquacious—none more so than Mr.
Scogan, the cynical middle-aged philosopher, a personage
destined to re-appear in many later novels. Here, for
instance, is Mr. Scogan's improvisation on the titles of
the dummy books which cover a door in the library of
the Wimbushs' country house :

" *Coffee-cup in hand, Mr. Scogan was standing in front of
the dummy book-shelf. Between sips he discoursed.*

" ' *The bottom shelf*', *he was saying,* ' *is taken up by an
Encyclopaedia in fourteen volumes. Useful, but a little dull,
as is also Caprimulge's* " *Dictionary of the Finnish Language*".
The " *Biographical Dictionary* " *looks much more promising.*
" *Biography of Men who were Born Great* ", " *Biography
of Men who Achieved Greatness* ", " *Biography of Men who
had Greatness Thrust upon Them* ", *and* " *Biography of
Men who were Never Great at all* ". *Then there are ten
volumes of* " *Thom's Works and Wanderings* ", *while* " *The
Wild Goose Chase* ", *a Novel, by an anonymous author,
fills no less than six. But what's this ? What's this ?* '
Mr. Scogan stood on tiptoe and peered up. ' *Seven volumes
of the Tales of Knockespotch. The Tales of Knockespotch* ',
he repeated. . .

" ' *Ah, my dear Henry* ', *he said, turning round,* ' *these are
your best books. I would willingly give all the rest of your
library for them . . .* '

" ' *I like the idea of the Biographies* ', *said Denis.* ' *There's
room for us all within the scheme ; it's comprehensive* '.

" ' *Yes, the Biographies are good, the Biographies are*

excellent', Mr. Scogan agreed. ' I imagine them written in a very elegant Regency style . . . perhaps by the great Dr. Lemprière himself . . .'

" ' I prefer " The Wild Goose Chase ", said Anne. ' A novel in six volumes—it must be restful '.

" ' Restful ', Mr. Scogan repeated. ' You've hit on the right word. A " Wild Goose Chase " is sound, but a bit old-fashioned—pictures of clerical life in the ' fifties ', you know ; specimens of the landed gentry ; peasants for pathos and comedy ; and in the background, always the picturesque beauties of nature soberly described . . .Personally, I like much better the notion of " Thom's Works and Wanderings ". The eccentric Mr. Thom of Thom's Hill. Old Tom Thom, as his intimates used to call him. He spent ten years in Tibet organizing the clarified butter industry on modern European lines, and was able to retire at thirty-six with a handsome fortune . . . And now we come to the " Tales of Knockespotch ".

" ' What a masterpiece and what a great man ! . . . . It was Knockespotch . . . the great Knockespotch, who delivered us from the dreary tyranny of the realistic novel. ' My life ', Knockespotch said, ' is not so long that I can afford to spend precious hours writing or reading descriptions of middle-class interiors !' He said again, ' I am tired of seeing the human mind bogged in a social plenum ; I prefer to paint it in a vacuum, freely and sportively bombinating ' . . . But it was only in his aphorisms that he was so dark and oracular. In his " Tales " he was always luminous. Oh, those Tales— those Tales ! How shall I describe them ? Fabulous characters shoot across his pages like gaily dressed performers on the trapeze. There are extraordinary adventures and still more extraordinary speculations. Intelligences and emotions, relieved of all the imbecile preoccupations of civilized life, move in intricate and subtle dances, crossing and re-crossing,

*advancing, retreating, impinging. An immense erudition and
an immense fancy go hand in hand. All the ideas of the
present and of the past, on every possible subject, bob up
among the " Tales", smile gravely or grimace a caricature of
themselves, then disappear to make place for something new.
The verbal surface of his writing is rich and fantastically
diversified. The wit is incessant. The . . .'*

" ' *But couldn't you give us a specimen* ', Denis broke
in—' *a concrete example ?* '

" ' *Alas !* ' Mr. Scogan replied, ' *Knockespotch's great
book is like the sword Excalibur. It remains stuck fast in this
door, awaiting the coming of a writer with genius enough to
draw it forth . . . The extraction of Knotchespotch from his
wooden prison I leave, my dear Denis, to you* '.

" ' *Thank you* ', said Denis ".

If the sword of Knockespotch was not definitely extracted by the appearance of Aldous Huxley's first novel,
at least there were indications that he might presently
draw it out. These hopes, however, were not realised
by the publication of its two successors—" Antic Hay "
in 1923 (the same year that saw the publication of T. S.
Eliot's " Waste Land ") and " Those Barren Leaves " in
1925. I still remember the disappointment that, twenty-
one years ago, " Those Barren Leaves " occasioned me.
What was my grievance ? On the surface at any rate,
the novelist remained as alert and intelligent as ever. He
tossed up ideas and caught them again with the same
bewildering facility. His digressions were as Knockes-
potchian. He tempered the realistic with the fantastic
as boldly, and almost as successfully, as he had done in
" Crome Yellow ". But the library-door had kept its
secret : the literary Excalibur slumbered. One noticed
—and this is a criticism that applies to all Aldous Huxley's

seven novels—that familiar well-worn characters kept perpetually popping up. The hero almost always proved to be an over-sensitive young man, deeply versed in art and literature but singularly maladroit in his relations with the opposite sex. He was tormented by a ' femme fatale ', whether it was Anne or Mrs. Viveash, and usually befriended and bothered by an eccentric aging hostess. And then, there was a cynical elderly man, whose disillusioned wisdom served as foil to the hero's romantic inexperience . . .

As for the writing—well, one could expect a passage on music, sometimes very beautiful, and several eloquent digressions on landscape, art and painting. Few novelists could give us so much. While I was looking around for a solution of my problem—Why did I enjoy the books of Huxley's later period far less than his 'prentice novel and the short stories assembled in " Limbo " and " Mortal Coils ? "—the novelist himself provided a characteristic and cogent answer.

In a pamphlet, published during 1930, entitled " Vulgarity in Literature ", I found the following incisive passage :

" *It was Flaubert, I think, who described how he was tempted, as he wrote, by swarms of gaudy images and how, a new St. Antony, he squashed them ruthlessly like lice against the bare wall of his study . . . The temptations which Flaubert put aside are, by any man of lively fancy and active intellect, incredibly difficult to be resisted. An image presents itself, glittering, iridescent ; capture it, pin it down, however irrelevantly too brilliant for its context. A phrase, a situation suggests a whole train of striking or amusing ideas that fly off at a tangent, so to speak, from the round world on which the creator is at work ; what an opportunity for saying some*

*thing witty or profound! True, the ornament will be in
the nature of a florid excrescence on the total work; but
never mind. In goes the tangent—or rather, out into artistic
irrelevancy. And in goes the effective phrase that is too
effective, too highly coloured for what it is to express; in
goes the too emphatic irony . . . For a self-conscious artist,
there is a most extraordinary pleasure in knowing exactly
what the results of showing off and protesting too much must
be and then (in spite of this knowledge, or because of it)
proceeding deliberately and with all the skill at his command
to commit precisely those vulgarities, against which his
conscience warns him and which he knows he will afterwards
regret. To the aristocratic pleasure of displeasing other
people, the conscious offender against good taste can add the
still more aristocratic pleasure of displeasing himself"*.

I can imagine no more pointed criticism of Aldous
Huxley's method.* Let us leave taste out of the question
and, for the moment, forget the word "vulgarity". I
recall an aphorism by Jean Cocteau. The artist, said
Cocteau, should possess "an inborn facility and an
acquired difficulty". He should subject his facility to
constant restraint : which, so far as I can make out, is a
course of action that Aldous Huxley may occasionally
have contemplated, but has very seldom practised. As
for the material he had to work on—Huxley's view of
life, in some ways remarkably extensive, is in others
strangely limited. He is apt at scoring off his personages.
But does he love or understand them ? He has none of
that wide sympathy—that gift of existing simultaneously
and intensely in several different characters—which we
find in the books of the great European novelists. He
is almost always *outside* the men and women he is
describing ; and when he seeks to penetrate their

epidermis the effect is so artificial as to seem sometimes rather clumsy. Then he descends to writing in clichés and employs the type of professional jargon best described as " novelese ".

At last, his facility exhausted itself : his intellectual progress came full circle—with consequences that are known to every modern reader. In 1930, he remarked of mystical writing that, being " *a literature about the inexpressible* ", it is " *for the most part misty indeed—a London fog, but coloured pink. It is only in the works of the very best mystical writers that the fog lifts—to reveal what ? A strange alternation of light and darkness : light to the limits of the possibility illuminable, and after that the darkness of paradox and incomprehensibility, or yet deeper, the absolute night of silence* ". Those infinite silences still alarmed him.

That was the day when, as an artist, he still loved the world and gloried, or appeared to *wish* to glory, in the simple fact of living. Than " the demonic energy of life ", he once informed us in an essay, nothing was more admirable—a conviction also voiced in a long rhapsodic poem entitled " The Cicadas ". Gradually the emphasis changed, as he drew near to the confines of the mysterious dusky universe inhabited by saints and mystics since the dawn of religious thought. And in his last novel, " Time Must Have a Stop ", the physical world has become a place of utter darkness. As a novel the book has merits. Huxley has recaptured some of the freshness and spontaneity of his earlier work in fiction. But the limitations of his point of view are more than ever obvious. The middle-aged cynic makes his bow for the fifth or the sixth time ; but he has lost all his saving graces, all his intellectual elegance ; even his habit of smoking cigars is described as if it were an obscene rite comparable to the Black Mass ! In the world that

Huxley now evokes there would appear to be no intermediate stage between the ecstatic and the repulsive: no allowance is made for harmless human pleasures, for the mild afternoon sunshine of ordinary human life : the writer is as implacable in his faith as he was once uncompromising in his scepticism : and the result is a courageous and original book, but one that, considered as a work of art, I believe to be a failure. I am still inclined to think of " Crome Yellow " and regret the " Tales of Knockespotch " . . . Excalibur remains embedded in the woodwork of the library door.

EVELYN WAUGH

by JOHN BETJEMAN

THERE IS NO LIVING NOVELIST whose works I
so thoroughly enjoy as those of Evelyn Waugh. I have
read all he has written twice and much of it three times.
Far be it from a cautious critic to say this man will last,
that one will be forgotten. But let me fling caution to
the winds and say that Evelyn Waugh is the one English
novelist of my own generation—that is to say of us who
are in the forties—who is certain to be remembered
while English novels are read.

About twenty-two new novels are published each
week. One in three hundred matters and that, probably,
not much. So let me beg his publishers to put him back
into print in a uniform edition worthy of a bookshelf—
the nine fiction books, the four travel books, the two
biographies and anything else they can collect. For each
of Evelyn Waugh's books is, to me at any rate, as a full
glass of dry, still champagne-wine—delicate, invigorat-
ing, uplifting and healthily purging.

I do not think it is just because Evelyn Waugh is of my
own world and age that he appeals to me. We have both
known Oxford of the 'twenties, schoolmastering,
country house life in England and Ireland, chattering

parties with the Bright Young Things in chromium flats,
and then piling into open cars to drive through midnight
London and bathe by the moon in a Middlesex pond.

No. That's not the reason. I think Evelyn Waugh
will last and will always appeal to those who like the
English language because he is a consummate user of it,
an accurate and learned observer a born storyteller and
possessed of a faultless ear for dialogue, finally because he
is a whole person with a complete philosophy of life.

Consider him as a craftsman. He does not *like*
writing, because, as his work shows, writing is to him
severe, even painful self-discipline. He will never use
two words where one is enough. He is the reverse of
gushing. So his books are short, and full. Take this
summary of a young author :

" *In the late twenties he set up as a writer and published
some genuinely funny novels on the strength of which he filled
a succession of rather dazzling jobs with newspapers and film
companies, but lately he had married an unknown heiress,
joined the Communist Party and become generally respectable*".

Indeed he is so " ungushing " that he is difficult to
quote, for the effect of one paragraph usually depends on
the one that precedes it. A good example of this comes
in " Vile Bodies ". Lord Balcairn the gossip writer had
been refused admittance to Lady Metroland's party. He
gate-crashed in a false beard but was turned out . . . and
put his head in a gas oven. He put a sheet of newspaper
on the tray, but noticed it was the gossip-page written by
his rival. In this passage, then, contrast the sordidness of
the first paragraph with the splendour of that which
follows.

" *He put in another sheet. (There were crumbs on the
floor). Then he turned on the gas ; it came surprisingly with a*

*loud roar ; the wind of it stirred his hair and the remaining
particles of his beard. At first he held his breath. Then he
thought that was silly and gave a sniff. The sniff made him
cough, and coughing made him breathe, and breathing made him
feel very ill ; but soon he fell into a coma and presently died.
" So the last Earl of Balcairn went, as they say, to his
fathers,—who had fallen in many lands and for many causes
as the eccentricities of British Foreign Policy and their own
wandering natures had directed them ; at Acre and Agincourt
and Killiecrankie, in Egypt and America. One had been
picked white by fishes as the tides rolled him among the treetops
of a submarine forest ; some had grown black and unfit for
consideration under tropical suns ; while many of them lay in
marble tombs of extravagant design ".*

Every novel of Evelyn Waugh's is packed with
significant description, almost feminine in its " catty "
observation of detail, but never, as one finds in so much
sensitive writing by women, too long.

Listen to this account, from " Scoop ", of the interior
of a daily newspaper office and the approach to the
sanctum of its full-blooded and alarming proprietor,
Lord Copper.

*" The carpets were thicker here, the lights softer, the
expressions of the inhabitants more careworn. The typewriters
were of a special kind ; their keys made no more sound than
the drumming of a Bishop's finger-tips on an upholstered prie-
dieu . . . At last they came to massive double doors, encased
in New Zealand rosewood which by their weight, polish and
depravity of design, proclaimed unmistakeably, ' Nothing
but Us stands between you and Lord Copper ' ".*

Notice the use of that word ' depravity ' at just the
right moment. I have been hard put to it to choose which
of about nine extracts I have made from his books will

best illustrate him. For Evelyn Waugh has this gift of story-telling, of holding your attention so that every word sparkles in its setting, and greedy, you reach forward for the next. I wish also to demonstrate that ear for dialogue which raises Evelyn Waugh above almost all living novelists. He has met so many types of people from natives in the jungle of British Guiana to motor salesmen in Great Portland Street, from commercial travellers to eccentric peers, from dyspeptic schoolmasters to social climbers and drunk journalists. He can catch the conversations of each in two sentences of dialogue. Should I quote that description of the school sports day from " Decline and Fall " when one of the masters shoots little Lord Tangent in the foot with the starting pistol ? Or the account of the coming of the diplomatic bag full of contraband goods to the remote British Legation in Africa in " Black Mischief ? " . . . or the way in which in " Put Out More Flags ", Basil Seal foists an unwanted and dirty family of "evacuee" children on super refined country families ? Or that infinitely touching account of the death of little John Andrew by a fall from a horse in a " Handful of Dust " ? Or should it be the poison distilled by Anthony Blanche, the Oxford aesthete in " Brideshead Revisited " ?

I decide on the description of the motor races from " Vile Bodies " not because that is his best book, but because it's easily available for those who wish to re-read it, and because it describes a variety of people and is a story in itself.

I am starting from that part in the story where Four Bright Young Things, the rich Archie Schwert, the outrageous Agatha Runcible, daughter of Lord Chasm, normal Adam Fenwick Symes, and the abnormal Miles Malpractice go down to a motor race in a provincial

town where Miles has a " friend " who is a racing driver.
They go on to the course where Miles' friend is listening
to the engine :

" *Miles' friend, even had it been possible in the uproar,
seemed indisposed to talk. He waved abstractedly and went on
with his listening. Presently he came across and shouted :*

" ' *Sorry I can't spare a moment, I'll see you in the pits.
I've got you some brassards*'.

" ' *My dear, what can that be ?* '

" *He handed them each a strip of white linen, terminating
in tape. 'For your arms', he shouted. 'You can't get into
the pits without them*'.

" ' *My dear, what bliss ! Fancy their having pits*'.

" *Then they tied on their brassards. Miss Runcible's
said, 'Spare Driver' ; Adam's, 'Depot Staff' ; Miles',
'Spare Mechanic' and Archie's 'Owner's Representative*'.

" *Up till now the little boys round the rope had been
sceptical of the importance of Miss Runcible and her friends,
but as soon as they saw these badges of rank they pressed
forward with their autograph books. Archie signed them
all with the utmost complaisance, and even drew a slightly
unsuitable picture in one of them. Then they drove away in
Archie's car. . . .*

" ' *The pits' turned out to be a line of booths, built of wood
and corrugated iron immediately opposite the Grand Stand.
Many of the cars had already arrived and stood at their 'pits',
surrounded by a knot of mechanics and spectators ; they seemed
to be already under repair. Busy officials hurried up and down,
making entries in their lists. Over their heads a vast loud
speaker was relaying the music of a military band. . . .*

" *Miss Runcible and her party found their way to the pit
numbered* 13 *and sat on the matchboard counter smoking and
signing autograph books. An official bore down on them.*

" ' *No smoking in the pits, please* '.

" ' *My dear, I'm terribly sorry. I didn't know* '.

" *There were six open churns behind Miss Runcible, four
containing petrol and two water. She threw her cigarette over
her shoulder, and by a beneficent attention of Providence, which
was quite rare in her career, it fell into the water. Had it
fallen into the petrol it would probably have been all up with
Miss Runcible.*

" *Presently No. 13 appeared. Miles' friend and his
mechanic wearing overalls, crash-helmets, and goggles, jumped
out, opened the bonnet and began to reconstruct it again.*

" ' *They didn't ought to have a No. 13 at all* ', *said the
mechanic. ' It isn't fair* '.

" *Miss Runcible lit another cigarette.*

" ' *No smoking in the pits,* please ', *said the official.*

" ' *My dear, how* awful *of me. I quite forgot* '.

" (*This time it fell in the mechanic's luncheon basket and
lay smouldering on a leg of chicken until it had burnt itself out*).

" *Miles' friend began filling up his petrol tank with the
help of a very large funnel.*

" ' *Listen* ', *he said. ' You're not allowed to hand me
anything direct, but if Edwards holds up his left hand as we
come past the pits, that means we shall be stopping next lap
for petrol. So what you've got to do is to fill up a couple of
cans and put them on the shelf with the funnel for Edwards to
take. If Edwards holds up his right hand . . .' elaborate
instructions followed. ' You're in charge of the depot* ', *he
said to Archie. ' D'you think you've got all the signals
clear ?   The race may depend on them, remember* '.

" ' *What does it mean if I wave the blue flag ?* '

" ' *That you want me to stop* '.

" ' *Why should I want you to stop ?* '

" ' *Well, you might see something wrong—leaking tank or*

anything like that, or the officials might want the number plate cleaned '.

" ' I think perhaps I won't do anything much about the blue flag. It seems rather too bogus for me '.

" Miss Runcible lit another cigarette.

" ' Will you kindly leave the pits if you wish to smoke ? ' said the official.

" ' What a damned rude man ', said Miss Runcible. ' Let's go up to that divine tent and get a drink '.

" They climbed the hill past the Boy Scouts, found a gate in the wire fence, and eventually reached the refreshment tent. . . . Then, refreshed, they returned to the course.

" By this time the cars were fairly evenly spread out over the course. They flashed by intermittently with dazzling speed and a shriek ; one or two drew into their pits and the drivers leaped out, trembling like leaves, to tinker with the works. One had already come to grief—a large German whose tyre had burst—punctured, some said, by a hireling of Marino's. It had left the road and shot up a tree like a cat chased by a dog. Two little American cars had failed to start ; their team worked desperately at them amid derisive comments from the crowd. Suddenly two cars appeared coming down the straight, running abreast within two feet of each other.

" ' It's No. 13 ', cried Miss Runcible, really excited at last. ' And there's that Italian devil just beside it. Come on, thirteen ! Come on ! ' she cried, dancing in the pit and waving a flag she found at hand. ' Come on. Oh ! Well done, thirteen '.

" The cars were gone in a flash and succeeded by others.

" ' Agatha, darling, you shouldn't have waved the blue flag '.

" ' My dear, how awful. Why not ? '

" ' Well, that means that he's to stop next lap '.

" ' Good God. Did I wave a blue flag ? '

" ' *My dear, you know you did* '.

" ' *How shaming.   What* am *I to say to him ?* '

" ' *Let's all go away before he comes back* '.

" ' *D'you know, I think we'd better.   He might be furious, mightn't he ?   Let's go to the tent and have another drink— don't you think, or don't you ?* '

" *So No.* 13 *pit was again deserted.* . . .

" ' *Let's go back and look at the motor cars,*' *said Archie.*

" They went down the hill feeling buoyant and detached (as one should if one drinks a great deal before luncheon).   When they reached the pits they decided they were hungry.   It seemed too far to climb up to the dining tent, so they ate as much of the mechanic's lunch as Miss Runcible's cigarette had spared.

" Then a mishap happened to No. 13.   It drew into the side uncertainly, with the mechanic holding the steering wheel. A spanner, he told them, thrown from Marino's car as they were passing him under the railway bridge, had hit Miles' friend on the shoulder.   The mechanic helped him get out, and supported him to the Red Cross tent.   ' May as well scratch ', he said.   ' He won't be good for anything more this afternoon. It's asking for trouble having a No. 13 '.   Miles went to help his friend, leaving Miss Runcible and Adam and Archie staring rather stupidly at their motor car.   Archie hiccoughed slightly as he ate the mechanic's apple.

" Soon an official appeared.

" ' What happened here ? ' he said.

" ' Driver's just been murdered ', said Archie.   ' Spanner under the railway bridge.   Marino '.

" ' Well, are you going to scratch ?   Who's spare driver ? '

" ' I don't know.   Do you, Adam ?   I shouldn't be a bit surprised if they hadn't murdered the spare driver, too '.

" ' I'm spare driver ', said Miss Runcible.   ' It's on my arm '.

" ' She's spare driver.   Look, it's on her arm '.

" ' Well, do you want to scratch ? '

" ' Don't you scratch, Agatha '.

" ' No, I don't want to scratch '.

" ' All right. What's your name ?'

" ' Agatha. I'm the spare driver. It's on my arm '.

" ' I can see it is—all right, start off as soon as you like '.

" ' Agatha ', repeated Miss Runcible firmly as she climbed into the car. ' It's on my arm '.

" ' I say, Agatha ', said Adam. ' Are you sure you're all right ? '

" ' It's on my arm ', said Miss Runcible severely.

" ' I mean, are you quite certain it's absolutely safe ? '

" ' Not absolutely safe, Adam. Not if they throw spanners. But I'll go quite slowly at first until I'm used to it. Just you see. Coming too ? '

" ' I'll stay and wave the flag ', said Adam.

" ' That's right. Good-bye . . . goodness, how too stiff-scaring . . . '

" The car shot out into the middle of the road, missed a collision by a foot, swung round and disappeared with a roar up the road.

" ' I say, Archie, is it all right being tight in a car, if it's on a race course ? They won't run her in or anything ? '

" ' No, no, that's all right. All tight on the race course '.

" ' Sure ? '

" ' Sure '.

" ' All of them ? '

" ' Absolutely every one—tight as houses '.

" ' That's all right then. Let's go and have a drink '.

" So they went up the hill again, through the Boy Scouts, to the refreshment tent.

" It was not long before Miss Runcible was in the news.

" ' Hullo, everybody ', said the loud speaker. ' No. 13, the English Plunket-Bowse, driven by Miss Agatha, came into

K

*collision at Headlong Corner with No. 28, the Italian Omega
car, driven by Captain Marino.   No. 13 righted itself and
continued on the course.   No. 28 overturned and has retired
from the race'.*

" ' *Well done, Agatha* ', *said Archie.*

" *A few minutes later :*

" '*Hullo, everybody.   No. 13, the English Plunket-Bowse
driven by Miss Agatha, has just completed the course in nine
minutes forty-one seconds.   This constitutes a record for the
course*'.

" *Patriotic cheers broke out on all sides, and Miss Runcible's
health was widely drunk in the refreshment tent.*

" *A few minutes later :*

" ' *Hullo, everybody ; I have to contradict the announce-
ment recently made that No. 13, the English Plunket-Bowse,
driven by Miss Agatha, had established a record for the course.
The stewards have now reported that No. 13 left the road
just after the level crossing and cut across country for five
miles, rejoining the track at the Red Lion corner.   The lap has
therefore been disallowed by the judges*'.

" *A few minutes later :*

" ' *Hullo, everybody ; No. 13, the English Plunket-Bowse
car, driven by Miss Agatha, has retired from the race.   It
disappeared from the course some time ago, turning left instead
of right at Church Corner, and was last seen proceeding south
on the bye-road, apparently out of control* ".*

    . . . But you must read yourself how they found Miss
Runcible's car crashed against an old stone market cross
in a distant village, and how, at the end of the adventure
they " conveyed her to a nursing home in Wimpole

---

    * *This passage is printed as Mr. Betjeman quoted it in his broadcast talk.   There he
said : " . . it will give me as much pleasure to read it as I hope it will give you pleasure to
hear it.   The only sufferer will be Evelyn Waugh himself, if he is listening from that graceful
Palladian house of his among the knobbly hills of North-west Gloucestershire   For,
unfortunately, I've got to do a lot of skipping and a lot of condensing in my own words as I
read it ".*

Street and kept her for some time in a darkened room ".

I have left to the last the most important part of Evelyn Waugh's work, his mental and spiritual growth, his outlook on human life. Some critics, particularly those who are materialists or those who think that there is such a thing as " progress " and that everything is getting better and better, conclude that Evelyn Waugh is getting worse and worse. They reckon his latest novel, " Brideshead Revisited " his greatest failure, while I regard it as his greatest achievement. They see all those gifts of story telling, dialogue, observation and brief wit still there—there is even greater abundance than before—they are infuriated to find them used to support a *theme* which they regard as either reactionary or mad.

For there is no doubt that Evelyn Waugh's writing has remained on the surface, as witty as ever, but his books have a seriousness underlying them which is too strong for those who prefer the bubbles to the wine.

Consider, for a moment, Evelyn Waugh as a person. His father, Arthur Waugh, was a scholar and writer. His elder brother Alec is a novelist. So he, the youngest, is deeply read in the prose and art of the last century. In 1926 when all the " smart " were mad about Cezanne and " significant form ", Evelyn Waugh was interested in the then despised Pre-Raphelites and published a short book on them. He went to an Art school and in 1928 published an authoritative life of Rossetti. Through the brambles and dark forests of Pre-Raphaelite detail he plunged towards the lilypond of the nineties with its writhing roots. From here it was a short step to the works of Ronald Firbank, the one writer whose style may be said to have coloured Evelyn Waugh's prose. Firbank, who has never been fully appreciated, specialised in allusive dialogue. But the world of his marvellous

conversations was one of pure fancy, set in Ruritanian
baroque. Both " Decline and Fall " and " Vile Bodies ",
Evelyn's earliest novels, have much Firbankian fantasy.
But there is in them what there is not in Firbank—a
detestation of twentieth century life, that was stimulated,
no doubt, by his love of the century before. He shared
with Firbank a preoccupation with style. But Evelyn
Waugh is also pre-occupied with people.

" Vile Bodies " brought him success and with the
money, he set out to travel, especially to countries where
there were people comparitively untouched by so called
" civilisation "—South American jungle, Spain, Mexico,
Abyssinia. His return to England made urban life seem
detestable still . " A Handful of Dust " the most perfect
of his books within limits he prescribed for it, is a heart-
rending condemnation of twentieth century England.

It is the story of Tony Last, a country landowner—
the surname " Last " is in itself significant—and of the
intrusion of amoral London life into his peaceful marriage
to his attractive Brenda. Brenda is led away by lust and
the twittering thrill of a flat in London among people
who gossip about one another on the telephone from
bed every morning. She deserts her husband, her son
and her village for a rootless life of electric bells, daily
papers and *chic* restaurants. The final chapter is a series of
unbearably touching contrasts between Tony, exploring
the Amazon and Brenda, betrayed by her lover and
her smart friends in London. As one may expect Tony's
native South American Indians seem hardly less human
than Brenda's jazzy hangers on. This is the last word in
mortal misery, it is also Evelyn Waugh's last word on
the unhappiness one individual can inflict upon another.

In the year that " A Handful of Dust " was published
—1934—its author was received into the Roman Catholic

Church. Clergy and religious denominations had always been a prominent feature of his books. There was reason behind the decision. His interest in people is not merely in their income groups, age-groups, their economic status. Had it been, he would, like Roger Simmons in "Work Suspended" have "married an heiress, joined the Communist Party and become generally respectable." He is interested in why they were born and where they are going after death. So to his logical mind, the Roman Catholic Church, once he had accepted its premises provided a fully worked out philosophical system. Never a lover of this age he is now primarily chiefly interested in how people prepare for the next. His last novel, "Brideshead Revisited" (1945) is an astonishing achievement. For here all the skill of the novelist has gone to elaborating the theme.

He has managed to convey the complete poverty of success that is purely worldly, and the deep riches of poverty that is only in this world's goods. The young careerist Canadian, a British M.P., who races through the pages is no more than a clever ape, though he is doing well in the world of big business and knows all the latest news. The drunken Sebastian without stamina or ambition, a prey to the bottle and the flesh, is a fully grown person because he has a sense of sin and guilt and a live sense of Divine order of created things. I will always remember a remark Evelyn Waugh made when someone said to him that he did not like Lady Marchmain, Sebastian's mother in that book, a sincere rather humourless Roman Catholic all high principles and good works, "*You* may not like her. But God loves her".

The latest work of Evelyn Waugh differs wholly from that of almost all other modern novelists. For whereas they are generally concerned with the relations of one human being to another, or one set of human beings to another set, he is also concerned with the human mind and soul as part of the Divine creation.

As he himself said in his only autobiographical article I have ever read, one which appeared in the American Magazine " Life " :

" So in my future books there will be two things to make them unpopular : a pre-occupation with style and the attempt to represent man more fully, which, to me, means only one thing, man in his relation to God ".

T. F. POWYS

by LOUIS MARLOW

THEODORE FRANCIS POWYS, although he was
born in Derbyshire, is a West-countryman very thoroughly by adoption ; for he has lived nearly all his seventy
years in Somerset and Dorset. The scenes of all his novels
and short stories are laid in Dorset—in what has been
described as " a small coastal area between Weymouth
and Wareham ". His brother, John Cowper Powys, is
also essentially a West-countryman, and so was his
brother Llewelyn. The title of John Cowper's best
known novel is " A Glastonbury Romance " : and
Llewelyn has written " Somerset Essays " and " Dorset
Essays ".

I have not time to do more than merely indicate what
a remarkable, even phenomenal family, these Powyses
are ; these sons and daughters of a Victorian Somerset
clergyman. There were eleven of them : the three
whom I have mentioned have all attained marked
distinction as writers. Two other brothers, and one
sister, have published work of strikingly individual
quality. Another sister is distinguished as a painter,
while a third is a leading expert on lace in the United
States.

It would, I think, be hard to name any living writer who is more original than T. F. Powys. He is not a popular writer—perhaps he is too original to be popular, too strange and sometimes too disturbing. His vision of life is entirely his own ; so much so that one wants to coin a word for it and call it " Theodorian ". In his novels and short stories men and women and their concerns are always unwontedly shown in the light of "Theodorian" love and hatred, "Theodorian" irony, sadness, humour, malice, and pity. All his characters are Dorset villagers ; peasants, farmers, clergymen, squires ; but they all of them possess those unchanging and unchangeable human qualities found in men and women of every age and of every land. They are human as the characters of the Bible are human. And, like the characters of the Bible, they are shown in their relation to God.

" *Man* ", he writes in " Soliloquies of a Hermit ", " *is a collection of atoms through which pass the moods of God, —a terrible clay picture, tragic, frail, drunken, but always deep rooted in the earth, always with claws holding on to his life while the moods pass over him and change his face and his life every moment. The people of the earth are clay pieces that the moods of God kindle into life* ".

Nature, too, is apprehended by T. F. Powys in relation to God :

" *It is the spring, and the apple-blossom is beautiful because He is there in it. To love Him is the only good thing in this world. It does not matter if He is true ; He is beyond all Truth. All things have breath in Him : I feel Him in the earth. . . His love is a terrible love,—terrible and deep, hard for a man to bear ; I have lived in it, I know it* ".

" *I see the awful Majesty of the Creator come into our own Grange Mead, and lie down amidst a joyous crowd of buttercups and red clover*".

" Soliloquies of a Hermit " is a very early work of this writer's, but it is an important one, because it communicates directly his searchings after God, and his faith. It is a key to his later writings, it reveals the impulse that brought them into being. But he will be remembered chiefly for his novels, his short stories, and his fables. All his novels and short stories have something of the nature of a fable ; that is, they have an allegorical quality. You must not expect them to be realistic in the usual sense. His world is, as it were, set at some removes from reality, but it has always a true correspondence with reality, a symbolic or allegorical correspondence.

In T. F. Powys's work there is indeed a suggestion of Gothic art. His people are sometimes like gargoyles, and sometimes they are like sculptured saints ; they have the same interpretative relation to actual men and women that medieval images have, giving the same strange illumination, the same sense of good and evil. His loving and tender and indeed almost pious embrace of good necessitates his savage, ferocious, sometimes vindictive revelation of evil ; it compels the saturation of his consciousness with evil and with horror. You will find both poison and balm in his books. Dreadful maladies are there, and healing beauty.

We will take now a short passage from one of the Fables called " John Pardy and the Waves ". T. F. Powys once told me that he " liked best a story about ordinary people, and then, for something odd to come in ", which is just what is always happening in his own stories. In this Fable the waves of the Dorset sea are speaking to John Pardy :

" ' *We have lived, Mr. Pardy, for so long in our own eternal beauty, we have rocked for years without number the towering icebergs and the great ships, we have made sport for the sea-serpent and the monstrous whales, and we have rolled lazily in the wide empty spaces where God lives. We have spoken to Him, and now we are willing enough to talk to you. Indeed, we are not ashamed to say that we have often felt, even in God's company, both sad and lonely, so that sometimes we have crept inshore to see what was a-doing, approaching the shallows of the Bay of Weyminster in little inquisitive wavelets. There we have made merry with the bare feet of children, the rinds of bananas and the little paper tickets that are given to the holiday makers who hire the summer chairs* ".

You see how, in this passage, high beauty and common human things come together to be joined in a kiss of love. The Fables have been published under the title of " No Painted Plumage ". This is T. F. Powys's own favourite among his books.

In his recently published book, " Bottle's Path ", in the story called " A Suet Pudding ", there is horror and evil. Genial, bearded Mr. Brine, who has such pleasant manners and is so dainty, keeps a thick leather strap behind a door to beat his wife with. " I do keep something behind door that be a good foreman over she ".

Mr. Brine is crushed by a fir-tree and, after a week or two, it is clear that his injuries will prove fatal :

" ' *Ah, yes* ', the doctor said to Mrs. Brine, ' *he may eat anything he wishes now* '.

" ' *I have made a suet pudding* ', said Mrs. Brine, *looking down*, ' *and he wants to eat it—he eats so nicely, you know—* '

" *Mrs. Brine brought in the pudding and, putting pillows behind her husband, she bade him eat.*

" *Mr. Brine took a piece into his mouth and then another,
in his usual polite manner. But, upon chewing for a moment,
he threw out what he had in his mouth.*

" ' The suet's not cooked ', *he said fiercely,* ' *It's hard as
leather. Go down, and bring me what's hung behind the
door* '.

" *He turned viciously to Alice.*

" ' *Strip yourself bare* ', *he shouted.*

" *Alice Brine smiled upon him.*

" ' *The strap's in the pudding* ', *she said meekly,* ' *you've
been eating it* '.

" *Mr. Brine gasped, his rage convulsed him—but not his
rage alone, for another unseen hand held him and he lay
still* ".

A very characteristic story of T. F. Powys, both in
matter and in style, appears in a recent number of " The
West Country Magazine ". It is called " The Devil and the
Good Deed ". I must abridge it a good deal, so I cannot
give you the full effect of the art of this story as a whole ;
but the simplicity and the force of the style will, I think,
appear clearly. The tramp in the story is not really a
tramp ; you will soon know who he is. In " Mr.
Weston's Good Wine ", you may remember, Mr.
Weston is not really a wine-merchant, nor, in " Unclay ",
is John Death really a tailor. This is how the story of
" The Devil and the Good Deed " begins :

" *Mr. Piller stood by his gate. He looked towards the
Dodder church ; he expected at any moment to hear the bell
toll for John Fardy . . . A tramp was going by* ".

The tramp hears two women gossiping about John :

" ' *'Tis a wicked man old Fardy have been* ', *said Mrs.
Gear happily,* ' *an' me husband do say 'tis to hell 'e be going* '.

'John Fardy', she says, 'has lived twenty years in the old
shepherd's hut that be falling to pieces. John were a shepherd
once. He was turned off by Farmer Lord because he wouldn't
be moved. Farmer did want hut moved ten miles away, but
John were afraid they little flying birds who do build in hut
would never find their nest again if 'twas shifted so far. Farmer
did order Carter Tom to start 'is horse, but Shepherd did lay
'is own body down before they wheels. Farmer did send
horses to move hut by night, and when John did hear their
tramp 'e did go out 'imself and set Farmer's barn on fire.

"So Mr. Lord soon called they horses back to drag thrashing
engine away from barn. Then wold hut were forgotten.
Once out of prison, John did go to hut again, but no one do
bide there only they Summer birds. And 'tis in thik hut 'e
be a-dying'".

The tramp goes on to the Vicarage and hears the vicar
talking of how old John never came to church and had
been sent to prison for setting the farmer's barn on fire,
and of how he drank and used bad language.

" ' I fear much that the evil one will take old John tonight' ",
says the vicar.

The tramp then goes to John's hut, and, on his way,
" a nimble swallow flew around his head, darted away into
the sky, caught a gnat, and flew around him again with a swish
of her wings. The tramp was in a rage. He threw his hat at
the swallow, and showed upon his forehead two shining
horns".

He arrives at the hut. Mrs. Piller, who is nursing the
dying man, takes him for a relation of his.

" ' I am come for John ', said the tramp, in a terrible tone.
" Mrs. Piller was startled. ' 'Tis one of they preachers',
she muttered.

" *The tramp . . . threw open the door and entered.*

" *In a moment he was cast out, as if by a strong invisible hand . . . Mrs. Piller was surprised. 'Evidently', she thought, ' though John Fardy be a-dying, 'e don't like to be visited by relations'.*

" *She went to the hut and peeped in. A bird was nestling upon John's breast, his dying hand caressed it.*

" *''Tis thik swallow that do build in hut', said Mrs. Piller, impatiently, ' and most like there'll be bird's lice to clear up as well as death sweat'.*

" *John gave a little sigh and died.*

" *The swallow rose. She touched the dead man's lips, then she flew far out into the evening sky* ".

I do not claim that T. F. Powys is everybody's writer. Those who love his writings and are fascinated by them will perhaps always be in a minority. So will the readers of William Blake and John Donne. I believe that T. F. Powys's work will always be read, as Blake's and Donne's will be.

This book

was first published

in 1947 by

Sylvan Press Limited

24 Museum St., London, W.C.1.

Set in Monotype Bembo

printed by Allen Davies & Co., Ltd., Bristol

bound by Novello & Co., Ltd., London, W.1.

Made in Great Britain

27115
P